"*The Jesus I Wish I Knew in Hi[gh]* [...] vision in which older saints impart gospel-centered, biblical wisdom to adolescent youth. The authors will encourage, equip, and challenge you to live a humble, faithful, and dependent life upon Christ by providing relevant and scriptural teaching on a wide variety of issues faced by today's teenagers."

Brian Cosby, Senior Pastor of Wayside Presbyterian Church (PCA), Signal Mountain, Tennessee; author of over a dozen books, including *Giving Up Gimmicks: Reclaiming Youth Ministry from an Entertainment Culture*

"These are honest, sacred pages. The authors courageously unveil true and painful stories from their own high school days, and then they share how those experiences intersect with the gospel, the truest story of all. This book is a gift to its readers. Read it and be tenderly reminded of God's unrelenting love for you."

Drew Hill, Pastor; award-winning author of *Alongside: Loving Teenagers with the Gospel*

"There is great freedom and joy to be found in following the Jesus of the Bible instead of limping after a counterfeit Jesus that the world has constructed. *The Jesus I Wish I Knew in High School* is a road map to the authentic Jesus and will serve as an encouragement for many teens to know that they are not alone and that they are loved beyond measure by their Creator!"

Barrett Jones, Former NFL player; Outland Trophy winner; college football analyst for ESPN Radio

"Students love relatable stories because not only do they help truth come to life, but they help teenagers realize they aren't alone. Most storytellers either seek to entertain or impress, but this book shines the spotlight on Jesus. I believe that these short chapters can help students make sense of the world around them and give them courage to share their own story with others."

Chris Li, High School Ministry Director, Mariners Church

"I wish I could have read *The Jesus I Wish I Knew in High School* when I was a teenager. This is an ideal handbook for parents, students, and teachers, with practical conversation starters and discussion questions on everything from cultural identity to ableism, gender, faith, and more. Through gospel-centered teaching and relatable storytelling, this book will both inspire and equip the next generation to love Jesus more and better understand Jesus's love for them."

Michelle Ami Reyes, Vice President, Asian American Christian Collaborative; author of *Becoming All Things: How Small Changes Lead to Lasting Connections Across Cultures*

"The first time I grasped the truth and power of the gospel was when I saw unexpected joy in my teenage peers. I wanted to know this Jesus who seemed so different, so alive compared to the stained-glass version I saw from the back of my church. I'm so grateful that another generation of youth will come to know this risen Christ through the testimonies of this creative and welcome book."

Collin Hansen, Vice President of content and editor in chief of *The Gospel Coalition*; host of the *Gospelbound* podcast

"It's been said that 'wisdom comes from experience.' I know that to be true, as over the course of my life I've learned to listen and learn from those who have gone before me who desired to faithfully follow Jesus. *The Jesus I Wish I Knew in High School* is packed with words of wisdom that have been born out of the experience of those who, like you and me, have desired to be faithful followers of Jesus Christ. Read and treasure these words from my friends. They understand what you're going through. Even more, they offer biblically faithful advice on how to get through it."

Walt Mueller, Center for Parent/Youth Understanding

"I want all young people to understand who Jesus is and how Jesus can change their life. This book strips away some of the (often well-intentioned) myths young people have absorbed about Jesus and keeps them ruthlessly focused on the true Jesus. The true Jesus is always compelling."

Kara Powell, Executive Director of the Fuller Youth Institute; Chief of Leadership Formation at Fuller; coauthor of *3 Big Questions That Change Every Teenager*

THE JESUS I WISH I KNEW IN HIGH SCHOOL

Edited by
Cameron Cole and Charlotte Getz

New
Growth
Press
newgrowthpress.com

New Growth Press, Greensboro, NC 27401
newgrowthpress.com
Copyright © 2021 by Cameron Cole and Charlotte Getz

Cover Design: Patrick Mahoney, themahoney.com
Interior Design and Typesetting: Gretchen Logterman

ISBN: 978-1-64507-149-5 (Print)
ISBN: 978-1-64507-150-1 (eBook)

Library of Congress Cataloging-in-Publication Data on file
LCCN 2021017781 (print) | LCCN 2021017782 (ebook)

Printed in India

29 28 27 26 25 24 23 22   2 3 4 5 6

Cameron Cole:

To Dad, who taught me that what truly mattered in life is trusting Jesus for salvation and being a humble Christian man.

Charlotte Getz:

To my parents, who always aimed me toward Jesus, in high school and beyond.

Contents

Introduction

Have you ever heard an adult say, "Just wait until you get into the real world" or "You think this is bad? Just wait until you're an adult"? Even if they don't say it out loud, you have probably noticed that it's easy for some adults to minimize the struggles of teenagers, and act as if "real problems" only begin when you hit the "real world." Too often we adults can be guilty of looking back at our lives through rose-colored glasses—only remembering the happy times from the past and forgetting the hard times.

Let us tell you the truth. If any adult sits down and does a sensible analysis of their entire life, they will agree that adolescence is universally the most difficult phase. When we ask other adults to really think about their teenage years, we often hear: "Man, being a teenager is brutal. That was the hardest time of my life. I can't imagine how hard it must be now."

As a teenager, you are starting to carry many of the expectations of adulthood, but without many of the benefits. You are expected to take responsibility for your grades, schedules, jobs, and applications like an adult, but you only receive limited freedoms in return.

Meanwhile, you are experiencing dozens of new and complicated challenges all at once. Your body is changing rapidly in ways that make you feel uncomfortable and insecure. You inch closer and closer to leaving home and are expected to make yourself marketable and attractive to potential employers or colleges. You gain the right to drive. You have more access to technology. Social groups and friendships change and evolve. You might have new financial responsibilities and obligations.

Adolescence is a hurricane, a tornado, an earthquake, and a forest fire coming at you all at once. As a result, many teenagers experience anxiety, stress, despair, and loneliness.

We get it. We remember.

Now, don't get us wrong. Being a teenager isn't all bad. There are games, parties, proms, pep rallies, and concerts. There can be great friendships, cool adventures, new learning experiences, and gratifying accomplishments. Being a teenager can be a thrill and a blast as well. The challenges, though, can be overwhelming.

WE WANT YOU TO KNOW TWO THINGS

The thirty volunteer authors of this book know two things, and we want you to take these two things to heart. First, we know that being a teenager is hard. Perhaps the hardest thing about it is that amidst the struggle, you feel as if other people in your life do not understand the gravity of the challenges and intensity of the difficulties you face. Part of the loneliness of adolescence is feeling constantly misunderstood and sensing that nobody takes your problems seriously.

One of the purposes of this book is for a group of Christians to affirm, "We hear you. We understand. We get the difficulty of what you are facing." That is why much of this book focuses on the authors sharing their own fears, failures, and struggles during their teenage years. We expect that as you read, you'll laugh, relate, and grow.

The authors range in age from twenty-three to seventy, but the fears, desperation, self-loathing, insecurity, embarrassment, conflict, and heartbreak are still very fresh to all of us. We hope that as you read, you will feel valued and understood. We want you to know that we take your struggles seriously.

The second and most important thing is that we want this book to point you to Jesus. When you know Jesus, you know what it's like to be perfectly loved, because Jesus loves you so much that he died for you. You know what it's like to have hope for the future, because you're confident that God has a plan for your life. You know what it's like to feel grace and mercy when you mess up big time, because forgiveness flows out of Jesus. And you know what it's like to have joy, because relationship with Christ is the source of all joy.

You cannot avoid pain and challenges in life. Those come with the territory. With Christ, however, you can walk through those challenges with greater hope and freedom.

WHAT'S IN THIS BOOK

The chapters are short and can be read within ten minutes. Each chapter has three sections. In the first section, the author shares a difficult experience they encountered in high school. The second section, *The Jesus I Wish I Knew*, contains a reflection from Scripture. The author considers how knowing Jesus and the gospel could have impacted his or her experience. In the final section, *The Jesus I Want You to Know*, the author speaks directly to you. Imagine they are sitting right beside you, sharing their heart. At the end of each chapter you will find optional questions for further reflection.

We want you to be filled with hope, peace, joy, and freedom. We want you to have Christ at the very center of your life, because he is the only place where we find true, abundant life.

From the Editors,
Cameron and Charlotte

Chapter 1
Temptation and Goodness
by Jen Pollock Michel

He is sixteen and I am fifteen. We're in the bedroom of a stranger's apartment with the lights off. The couple we've come with has paired off in the other bedroom. At some point, my boyfriend reaches over me, fumbling to open the drawer of the nightstand beside us. He closes it, holds a small foil-wrapped package in the palm of his hand. There is a single suspended moment of indecision.

And then there is not.

I was raised in church, knelt beside my mother at the age of six to ask Jesus to live in my heart. There was little I didn't *know* about Jesus, at least as I thought then, and there was nothing I openly rejected. I'd believed in Jesus my whole life: believed that he was God in the flesh, believed that he died on the cross for my sins, believed that he was raised from the dead—I even believed that he was coming again.

At fifteen, I didn't mind believing in Jesus, didn't even mind most of the Sunday mornings my parents drug me out of bed early for church. I just didn't want Jesus ruining my fun or restricting my freedoms. I was like the prodigal son in Luke 15—simply looking for a good time. I planned, of course, to come "home" at some point. I knew I'd need to make sincere apologies and promises to God when I did. But I was postponing that repentance for a later date: after thirty maybe, when life would find me behind the wheel of a minivan. Following Jesus was like paying the mortgage—and having a lawn to mow.

For a year, my boyfriend and I played married. Ironically, we also used to entertain long theological conversations about the state of our souls. He, too, had been raised in the church, and neither of us had any hesitation about the sinfulness of our behavior. Still, we lingered over this question: Were we—or were we not—Christians? My favorite verse as a child was Ephesians 2:8: "For by grace you have been saved through faith. And this is not of your own doing; it is the gift of God." I counted on pardon and felt sure that however much I tested God's steadfast and abounding love, it would never break under me.

It might have continued on like that except that I discovered this to be true of God: he is a loving shepherd seeking the stray.

For one, I was surrounded by people who loved Jesus in very real ways. Their sincerity was a foil to my hypocrisy. Aside from my parents, there was my Sunday school teacher: a single woman whose lessons were her life. She radiated a joy deeper than anything I recognized from my Saturday nights. There was a friend from church, a girl one year older than me, who attended a different high school. She read her Bible during the week as if the words of God really mattered, and she pursued a holiness—an *otherness*—that I found myself admiring. These examples of faith stirred longing in me—for something more solid, more stable than the sand beneath my feet.

If you know the story of Saul on the road to Damascus in the book of Acts—this fire-breathing man with arrest warrants for Christians in his hand, this man who met the blazing spectacle of the risen Jesus one ordinary afternoon—then you might not be surprised when I tell you that I also met Jesus when I least expected to. I was sixteen when I heard his voice at summer camp, asking me three questions: *What do you want? Where are you headed? Will you follow?*

I don't remember indecision then, only the urgency of *yes*.

THE JESUS I WISH I KNEW IN HIGH SCHOOL

This story of mine is now thirty years old, and there's a lot I've left out: the breakup, the rebuilding, how my new friendship with Jesus filled all the lonely places. In truth, it's not a story about sex as much as it is about surrender. It's a story about temptation, and it's a story about trust. It's a story about coming home to a Father—and finding him good.

I think of one of the oldest stories in the Bible, found in Genesis. It's the story of our human parents, Adam and Eve, and recounts the day they mistrusted God. God had, of course, lavished all of his best gifts on these children of his, and there was nothing they lacked, even if there was one thing he had forbidden them. "You may surely eat of every tree of the garden, but of the tree of the knowledge of good and evil you shall not eat, for in the day that you eat of it you shall surely die" (Genesis 2:16–17). We can't be exactly sure why God would cordon off this one tree, but it does confront Adam and Eve with two very important questions, especially as the serpent cast suspicion on God's motives. *Is God good? Can God be trusted?*

In the midst of their temptation, they had to decide what they believed about God's nature and where they would find life's purpose.

At fifteen, I wish I'd had better answers to these questions. At fifteen, I thought of God as stingy, as always standing in the way of a good time. I knew that he was *God*—and that being God, he expected to be obeyed. But I thought surrendering myself to him meant signing up for a life I didn't really want, a life that would always look like the cheap knockoff version of the better life everyone else would be living. It's not hard to see why Adam and Eve—and every human since—has been grabbing for the things God forbids. We just aren't convinced that he's good. We think of his commands as prohibitions and punishments instead of invitations to *life*.

I had all the wrong ideas about following Christ at fifteen, but when I finally decided to follow him, I began believing in his goodness. I risked that I'd find my best life in him. Let me tell you, friends: it's the surest bet I've ever placed.

It seems crazy that we'd find it so hard to believe in God's goodness, given that the one Bible verse we are all supposed to have memorized—the one Bible verse most widely known—is a verse about God's generous giving. "For God so loved the world, that he gave his only Son" (John 3:16a). I wish I'd grasped what this meant for the apostle Paul, who saw the cross of Christ as a display of God's goodness and generosity, his grace toward his people. "He who did not spare his own Son but gave him up for us all, how will he not also with him graciously give us all things?" (Romans 8:32). Paul wanted his readers to stare long and hard at the self-sacrifice of God. He wanted us to see the innocent God-Man, who allowed himself to be beaten, tortured, and executed for the sake of love. He wanted us to doubt our doubts about God and then ask, *Does that look like stinginess to you?*

If God is stingy, then life will always require the stealing that took place in the garden. If God is stingy, we can't count on him to give us what we need, to lead us into the good life. We'll have to take it for ourselves. But if God is good, if God is generous, if God is so lavish in love that he'd suffer torture for our sakes, we can lean into trusting his direction for our lives, lean into knowing that every "no" has a purpose and leads us toward life in Christ.

In the words of a song I sang as a child, we can "trust and obey."[1]

THE JESUS I WANT YOU TO KNOW

The word *gospel* means good news, and that's what I want to leave with you. You might think you *lose* your life in order to follow Jesus, but let me assure you: in the end, you ultimately *find* it. At fifteen, I started to understand what Paul meant in Philippians 3, when he said that everything was loss compared to knowing Christ.

I wonder if you, if I, can't start trying to trust that God's Word is good, that God's plans are good, that God's providence

---

1. John H. Sammis and Daniel B. Towner, "Trust and Obey" (Public Domain, 1887), https://hymnary.org/text/when_we_walk_with_the_lord.

is good. In the words of the psalmist who speaks to God, "You are good and do good; teach me your statutes" (Psalm 119:68). I think faith—obedient faith—hangs on this promise, and that's what I want to see formed in you.

Can I give you just one (lifelong) assignment? It's extraordinarily easy and difficult at the very same time. It's simply this: to try learning the height, the depth, the width, and the length of God's love "that [we] may be filled with all the fullness of God" (Ephesians 3:19b). If he truly is perfectly, generously good, why would we not follow?

DEVOTIONAL QUESTIONS

Read Romans 8:31–32.

1. This passage contains three characteristics about God. What are they?
2. The author of chapter 1 describes how she came to understand God's goodness. Consider a time when you were tempted to question his goodness.
3. What are some obvious and not-so-obvious ways in which God has been good and generous to you?

SURRENDER (verb): To release control completely. To give in to the power of another.

What this means for you: Christ calls you to *surrender*—to give him complete control of your life. You can let go of the reins. You can rest. You can trust God is good.

Chapter 2
Performance and Acceptance
by Cameron Cole

"This grade is going to be on your permanent record. Colleges will see this."

I remember that oft-repeated phrase that teachers reiterated, starting in the ninth grade. It created a sense of dread and anxiety deep in my gut with each pronouncement. I perceived that teachers were holding it over our heads, as if they held the key to the door of our futures.

Prior to high school, we played after school with foam sabers, but now the stakes were raised: now it seemed like we were playing with real swords. What this meant to me was that every assignment—every test, every quiz, every paper, every homework grade—had bearing and determination over my future. One slip-up, one off day, one unit of math that I didn't understand, one week of missed school, one week of slacking off and—*Boom!*—my college dreams would explode into a million pieces of shattered glass. A single mediocre mark on my résumé would destroy all of my hopes for the future.

This pressure resulted in a persistent undercurrent of anxiety that was so ever-present it became as normal as breathing. Fear pervaded my life. School felt like the grounds where my entire future depended on my performance on every single test and every single assignment. I carried the weight that only God could carry.

The ugliness of this pressure manifested itself my sophomore year, when I got my first "F" on a chemistry test. The 44 written in bright red ink revealed my profound inadequacy.

When a vessel contains so much heat and energy and pressure and it builds, and builds, and builds, what happens? It explodes.

I exploded.

I took the test paper, crushed it inside my intensely clenched fist, then unraveled the small wad and tore it into a hundred pieces. With the teacher watching. My stunned classmates— eyes wide open—watched their nice, well-mannered peer transform into a total enraged psycho.

To whom was my fury directed? Not the teacher. Not God. Not my classmates. *I* was the object of my own wrath. I poured down judgment on myself as I screamed under my breath.

You stupid idiot. You moron. You are such a stupid piece of trash. How could you be so dumb. I hate to admit it, but the words I used to describe myself were far more profane than that.

I wasn't even embarrassed at my toddler-style tantrum and my profanity-laced self-shaming. To me, my inadequacy was so flagrantly obvious that I couldn't understand why my outrageous reaction surprised my peers.

The pressure and performance all pointed in one direction: my college résumé. In the fourth grade, after placing in the top five in the southeastern United States in the 100-yard backstroke, I asked my mother if I could put this accolade on my college résumé. Even in elementary school, the culture had ingrained this formula in my head: life is for building your college résumé, your college résumé is for getting into the highest ranked school possible, the highest ranked school possible is for ensuring a life of happiness. We all knew the inversion of this formula: failure to build a satisfactory résumé means failure to attend top-ranked school, which means failure in life itself. To attend a mediocre college or (God forbid) to not attend college at all certainly meant you would spend most of your adult life sleeping in a gutter.

Résumé-building consumed my life. Every activity had to be added to this growing document. Every waking minute involved studying or extracurriculars. I even invested time between events at swim meets studying vocabulary for the SAT. High school life was a four-year, all-consuming strategy, with a goal of optimizing maximal acceptances to as many *U.S. News and World Report Top 25* colleges as possible.

As a result, every single endeavor took on life-and-death stakes because, in my mind, my future happiness and well-being hinged on my performance in high school and on the quality of my résumé. Even though I did have a spectacular résumé and I did get into the highly-ranked college of my choice, I look back on my adolescent self as an unhappy person. I felt as if I lived in a locked closet, chained to a treadmill that never stopped running. I. Was. Miserable.

THE JESUS I WISH I KNEW IN HIGH SCHOOL

Résumés are not a modern invention, and they don't only relate to colleges and jobs. The apostle Paul listed his religious résumé in Philippians 3 when he wrote, "If anyone else thinks he has reason for confidence in the flesh, I have more: circumcised on the eighth day, of the people of Israel, of the tribe of Benjamin, a Hebrew of Hebrews; as to the law, a Pharisee; as to zeal, a persecutor of the church; as to righteousness under the law, blameless" (vv. 4b–6).

Before Paul came into a saving relationship with Jesus, he was a spiritual rock star in the Jewish faith. He had religious status through birth. As one circumcised on the eighth day, and of the people of Israel, he was a pure-blooded Jew, which meant something in those days. As a person born of the tribe of Benjamin, he was from the most prestigious of the Israelite clans. As a "Hebrew of Hebrews," this meant that his family spoke Hebrew, which was a status merit badge among Jews.

From a Jewish standpoint, people would have envied Paul's status. He was the kid from the "right" family. He reeked of impressiveness.

While the first half of the apostle's résumé contained attributes that he was born with, the second half had everything to do with his achievements. Paul practiced Judaism as a Pharisee, the strictest, most respected sect of Jews. As a persecutor of Christians, he demonstrated the highest passion and intensity. With regard to observing the law, his observance of the Jewish rituals and regulations neared perfection.

Paul earned the perfect religious résumé. If he were an athlete, he would have been All-American with dozens of scholarship offers and a chance to play in the pros. If he were a student, he would have had a 36 on the ACT, 5's on all of his AP test, and acceptances from Ivy League schools. If his thing had been social media popularity, he would've had 20,000 friends on Instagram and a YouTube channel with a million subscribers. He had reached the top.

But here's the problem: Paul was miserable.

However, like me, Paul never realized this until he tasted the freedom of the gospel and the joy of a relationship with Christ. When he turned his life over to Christ, he found a peace, hope, and love that he had never tasted before. He experienced such satisfaction that he deemed his past deeds as "rubbish" (or "dung," as some translators interpret it—see Philippians 3:8 csb).

In Paul's former life, he had to earn his righteousness every day. He had to win God's approval with each religious challenge. Each new day constituted a proving ground. Each moment a risk of falling from perfection into failure and shame.

I don't know about you, but I can relate to Paul. Every day as a teenager, I felt so much pressure to be impressive and I experienced so much fear of imperfection. Paul and I had two misunderstandings.

First: you may not realize this, but, because of our sinful nature, we all live with an impulse to create our own righteousness through performance. We all have this sense that we are not quite good enough. This sense is actually true. As sinners, *all people* "fall short of the glory of God" (Romans 3:23b). In order to enter into relationship with a holy God, we must have all of our sins washed away. We need his righteousness to cleanse us—so we can be completely loved and accepted by God.

All sinners have the same initial misunderstanding about righteousness. We try to earn it through performance, which we might pursue in sports, popularity, school, morality, or appearance. Where performance pressure exists, we try our best to succeed.

Second: my obsessive pursuit of the perfect college résumé was really just a manifestation of me trying to make myself "enough" in God's eyes and my own. It was me trying to manufacture my own righteousness. This striving exhausted me. Why? Because only God can make us righteous through grace.

I was a Christian. I had asked Jesus to be my Savior as a third grader. I attended church weekly, read my Bible, and shared the gospel with others. I primarily understood the gospel as my ticket into heaven. I *did not* realize that the gospel gave me peace, freedom, and comfort in this life.

This changed when my life of performance finally ran me into a spell of deep depression and anxiety. My pastor told me, "The gospel is rest. The gospel means Jesus carries the burden of your life. The gospel means you will never have to prove yourself again." For the first time in my life, I realized that I was enough. Jesus had given me his righteousness as a free gift. God had made me enough by grace through faith. And, like Paul, all my successes seemed like garbage compared to the peace and comfort of knowing the gospel of grace.

As I continued to grow in this truth, I no longer felt pressure to perform or to earn my own righteousness. I was able to remember, even in the midst of temptation, "I don't have to be impressive. Christ has made me enough."

THE JESUS I WANT YOU TO KNOW

What I wish I had known—and what I want for you—is to know that you are enough through Christ. You don't have to prove yourself. You don't have to impress anyone. If you trust in

God's grace through Jesus Christ, rather than your own spiritual performance, you will know the Lord has made you perfectly acceptable in his eyes. There is nothing more to prove.

Rest in comfort: through Christ, you are enough.

DEVOTIONAL QUESTIONS

Read Philippians 3:1–11.

1. What do you think Paul meant when he said, "Indeed, I count everything as loss because of the surpassing worth of knowing Christ Jesus my Lord" (v. 8a)?
2. The author of chapter 2 describes how true worth is rooted in the gospel. Describe the gospel. What does it mean to you?
3. In what ways do you feel like you are not enough? What things do you do to try to make yourself feel better? How can resting in the perfection and love of Jesus make a difference?

THE GOSPEL (noun): The good news of God's grace and redemption for sinners through the life, death, and resurrection of Jesus Christ. It is the primary message of the Bible and of Christianity.

What this means for you: When you trust the gospel, you can live freely before a God who delights in you. Because of Jesus, there is nothing you can or can't do that will make him love you any less.

Chapter 3
Grief and Empathy
by Mac Harris

My whole world skidded to a stop.

Moments earlier, I had been studying for a math quiz in the same room as my brothers and parents. Aside from the portable hospital bed, IV pumps, and life-support equipment keeping my dad alive in our basement, it might have looked like a normal scene.

But a series of coughs broke the stillness, and suddenly my brothers and I were rushed out of the room, whisked upstairs to sit in stunned silence with my uncles. My dad's year-and-a-half-long battle with cancer should have prepared me for that moment; instead, the reality of death paralyzed and swallowed me whole.

I was thirteen when my dad died, and I had all kinds of people lovingly tell me that I was going through something no kid should have to endure. But the truth is, the loss of a loved one is one of the few constants in life; death doesn't wait to strike until you're out of high school and "mature" enough to handle it.

So there I was, a grieving eighth grader with no idea how to grieve. My two younger brothers and I reacted in different ways—with anger, depression, withdrawal—and tried to cope with sports, academics, and anything that reminded us of dad. As the oldest, I felt a particular responsibility to be the "man of the house" (a hilarious notion when I think back), to care for my mom and brothers. I did everything I could to be like my dad, trying to hold onto his memory by emulating his love for college football, working hard in school, and cracking dry jokes.

At the same time, I hardened myself. In contrast to the tears and emotional outbursts of my mom and brothers, I thought I had to be the one who was tough and strong and steady. I had to bury my pain so deep that it couldn't resurface, hiding under layers upon layers of anything that would distract me from the emptiness I felt inside. I didn't want to feel weak, sad, or acknowledge that I had experienced a life-altering loss, so I projected a performance-based put-togetherness for all the world to see.

More than anything, however, this brave face obscured an emotional and spiritual numbness, as well as a chorus of doubts rattling around inside my head: *Maybe I should have prayed more. Why hadn't I spent more time with Dad? Can I even trust a God who let him die?*

While I tried to hide my scars, minimize my loss, and numb the pain, God graciously covered me with the love of other dad-like figures. Instead of mending my heart with one person, God blessed me with a youth pastor who welcomed me into fellowship, a high schooler who drove me to and from practices, and a friend's dad who sacrificed time to invest in me and my brothers.

As I tried to distract myself, God slowly but surely used these men to chip away at the defenses I had hastily constructed to cover my grief. I spent years burying my painful emotions and hiding from the real grief I never allowed myself to feel. But my senior year of college, my college minister sat me down for a moment of brutal honesty. In the midst of trying to figure out my plans for after graduation, he asked me a simple, surprising question: "Have you ever grieved the loss of your dad?"

I was taken aback and unsure why this was relevant. I stumbled over an answer and told him I was fine. After all, it had almost been a decade, and time heals all wounds, right? But he saw right through me. On a napkin (that I've kept to this day), he drew a crude (yet elegant) diagram of a canyon. Between where I was standing on one side of the canyon and where I wanted to go on the opposite side was a deep valley. Like Yoda sending Luke into the cave full of his fears in *The Empire Strikes Back*, my college pastor offered a simple yet invaluable lesson: to get to the new life and healing and joy that I desired, I had to go *through* the death and sorrow. I was stuck, trying to get to the other side, but unwilling to walk through the valley of the shadow of darkness.

I wanted to build a magical bridge and walk right over my hurt, but that's not the way of the Lord. Instead, he uses our scars and sorrows not for punishment, but to grow us and lead us, for it is "through many tribulations we must enter the kingdom of God" (Acts 14:22b).

THE JESUS I WISH I KNEW IN HIGH SCHOOL

A lifetime of Sunday school had taught me that the good news— the best news—was that Jesus could comfort me through this valley. But it was difficult to believe. How could he comfort me, here and now?

Like my campus minister said, God calls us to walk *through* the valley of the shadow of darkness and death. There's no way around it. But there's also no one-size-fits-all formula for grieving. Some days, I wanted nothing more than a hug from a friend. On other days, a simple kind word from my mom would send me over the edge. Sometimes, I found comfort hiding in a crowd, or felt even lonelier surrounded by friends who couldn't possibly understand what I was going through. I might be kept up at night by the suffocating straitjacket of loss, or wrestle with guilt for not feeling *more* heartbroken. The point is, no matter what our grieving looks like, we can't hide from it, but we also can't just wash it away with theological truths. We need something more.

The Christianity I knew in high school met me in my loss with the truths that God was good, and that he was sovereign over my sorrow. Well-intentioned friends and family tried to comfort me—with pity I rarely wanted—offering platitudes or cherry-picked verses like Romans 8:28: "And we know that for those who love God all things work together for good, for those who are called according to his purpose." And don't get me wrong: God is good, and he is sovereign, and these were truths that I needed to hear.

But faced with that chasm of darkness, they were not the only truths I needed to hear.

The notion that "God will turn your suffering into something good" is absolutely true, but if that's all you hear, it's an incomplete view of God. When we exclusively think of Jesus as the Son of God or King or Lord—all biblical and beautiful truths—we can lose sight of his tender, intimate, and loving humanity.

Our God isn't a distant and impersonal deity; rather, he humbled himself and took on our humanity (see Philippians 2:5–11). Jesus wasn't just any man, he was "despised and rejected by men, a man of sorrows and acquainted with grief" (Isaiah 53:3a). Jesus knows our deepest pain, loss, and grief because he lived each of those things.

Not only can he identify with our deepest hurt, but we know that his heart breaks when our hearts break. Though Jesus knew he was about to raise Lazarus from the dead, when he saw Mary's tears, he couldn't help but weep himself (see John 11:28–37). Think about that! The God and Savior of the world broke down in tears because his friend was grieving. The loneliness of loss can feel soul-crushing, but it is powerful to remember we are never crying alone.

As Dane Ortlund writes in his book *Gentle and Lowly*, "In our pain, Jesus is pained; in our suffering, he feels the suffering as his own even though it isn't."[1] And more than any of us, Jesus understands loss. Not only was he abandoned by the crowds, his family, and his friends, but Jesus experienced a cosmic loss that we cannot even begin to comprehend. "My God, my God, why have you forsaken me?" he cried from the cross, experiencing the separation and loss of his Father in heaven—an incomparable loneliness (Matthew 27:46b).

So in the most real, intimate, and loving way possible, Jesus promises to walk alongside us every step of the way. God not

---

1. Dane C. Ortlund, *Gentle and Lowly: The Heart of Christ for Sinners and Sufferers* (Wheaton: Crossway Books, 2020), 46.

only understands our pain, but he endures it with us. I wish I had known as a teenager that, even more than the best earthly friend or loved one, our God shoulders our burdens, weeps with us in our grief, and sits in our sorrow. When we need a tender touch, he draws near. When we want to curl up in isolation, he sits with us, holding our hand (see Psalm 73:23). When we want to vent to someone who understands, he lends a listening ear. Ortlund quips that Jesus "will never lob down a pep talk from heaven. He cannot bear to hold himself at a distance. Nothing can hold him back. His heart is too bound up with yours."[2]

THE JESUS I WANT YOU TO KNOW

I'm a lot closer to being in high school than many of the other writers here. As a result, I'm still learning how to navigate this whole "grief" thing along with you. But if you have lost a friend or a loved one, know you are not alone. Your story and your loss are real, and God doesn't want you to shrink away from it.

Instead, he invites you to walk through the muck and the mire of mourning and sit right in the emotions you wish you could escape. This isn't some trick or test of faith, but God's good purpose for healing and making all things new. In the midst of your grief and loss, I invite you to read the Psalms and cry out to God with the psalmist; cling to God, for he will uphold you (see Psalm 63:8). No matter how alone you feel, Jesus invites you to take him by the hand and wade into your sorrows together.

Finally, I want to encourage you in your prayers. Whether praying for yourself or for someone you love, know that God hears your prayers and that they have power. After my dad died, many people told me that God sometimes says "no" to phys-ical healing. While this is technically true, the Bible offers an even better hope: sometimes, God's answer is simply "not yet." One day, we know for certain that "he will wipe away every tear from their eyes, and *death shall be no more*, neither shall there be mourning, nor crying, nor pain anymore, for the former things

---

2. Ortlund, *Gentle and Lowly*, 50.

have passed away" (Revelation 21:4, emphasis mine). For many of us, God may have answered our prayers for healing differently than we imagined, but they have not fallen on deaf ears. Not only does Jesus comfort us in our grief today, but someday soon, God will complete his work of redemption. Our deepest pains will fade into a distant memory as we rejoice together in our resurrected, restored, and eternal bodies.

DEVOTIONAL QUESTIONS

Read Isaiah 53:3.

1. In this passage, the prophet describes the future sufferings of the Messiah, Jesus Christ. In what ways can you relate to the suffering described?
2. The author of chapter 3 describes how he tried to skip over the hard parts of grief. Jesus invites you to share the traumatic parts of your own story with him, that he might accompany you along the way. What might you share with him today?
3. What part of Jesus's life and death might give you assurance that he is trustworthy to carry your burdens?

SYMPATHY VS. EMPATHY (nouns): Having sympathy involves having compassion for another person, even though you can't identify with their suffering. Having empathy involves compassion *with* understanding. It is a shared experience.

What this means for you: Because Jesus is an empathetic God, he identifies with your struggles and pain. He understands your every weakness and invites you to draw near.

Chapter 4
Misfits and the Arrival of God
by Michelle Ami Reyes

My existence in high school sometimes felt like one extended experience of humiliation.

The boys in my grade had a running joke about the way I looked. One time, as I sat down in a classroom, a boy stood up and shouted, "Hey, look at Michelle! She's so ugly." Never in my life had I wanted to be more invisible than in that moment. I still remember the way all eyes turned to look at me, and an immediate roar of laughter erupted across the room. I heard one girl ask out loud, "Why are you so dark anyways?" Another guy leaned over and said, "You know no one's ever going to date you, right?" All I could do was hang my shoulders low and sink down as far as I could into my chair, hoping it would swallow me whole.

I was the lone brown-skinned Indian girl in an all-white town. No one in my school, my church, or my neighborhood looked like me or lived life like me. But I had the same desires as everyone else in high school: I wanted friends, I wanted to fit in, to be liked, maybe even to have a boyfriend.

The boy's words in class that day lingered with me: *you know no one's ever going to date you.* The boys in my grade had an awful ranking system. They openly discussed how pretty each of the girls were. They'd rank them and say who they would want to date first, second, etc. You get the picture. It was horrible. Boys should never treat girls in this way. Ever. Girls should never be reduced to sexual objects and valued because of their looks. Nevertheless, I was never included on these lists because of my brown skin. I'm glad *now* that I wasn't part of those lists, but back then I continually felt mortified that I was known as the ugly and un-dateable girl.

To make matters worse, some of the kids called me "Pocahontas," a name they hoped would make me feel insulted. I was the brunt of a sad joke, made sadder still by the fact that I was being misidentified for a Native American woman, and even worse that a Native American woman was used as a racial slur against me. None of this was okay.

Eventually, the shame was too much to bear and I started trying to hide my Indianness. I wore long-sleeved shirts to hide my arms. I stopped wearing traditional Indian clothes in public.

I also stopped bringing Indian food to lunch because my peers made fun of how it looked and smelled. This type of food-shaming is wrong and it continues today.

I told myself that hiding my real self was worth it. If I could figure out how to act like the cool kids, dress like the pretty girls, do my hair the way they did, or talk the way they did, then maybe my peers wouldn't make fun of me in class anymore, exclude me from parties, or say my culture was weird.

Unfortunately, this led to a different problem. When people first got to know me, they'd ask questions like, "You're sort of Indian, right?" My Indian friends and cousins would constantly tell me that I wasn't a true Indian. All of a sudden, I didn't know who I was anymore or how I was supposed to live my life. As a bicultural, second-generation Indian American, I wasn't fully Asian, but I wasn't really white either. I had no friends and, above all else, I didn't understand why God made me the way he did.

I *really* wish that someone would have told me in high school that who I was, as a bicultural Indian American girl, mattered. I wish I could have had a Bible as a kid that depicted Jesus as a brown-skinned man. I wish one of my pastors or Bible teachers would have told me that I was created with a beautiful,

God-given, cultural identity. I was born and raised in a Christian home and throughout high school I loved Jesus with all my heart. But I had no idea that Jesus was a brown-skinned person like me. I had no idea that he experienced similar insults and rejections during his life on earth. I wish that someone could have mapped this out for me when I was in high school, so that I could have looked to him for encouragement.

The Jesus I Wish I Knew in High School

My life has always been one of straddling fences and living in the in-between. Being Indian American means being a *mestizo*: a person in between worlds and never fully fitting in anywhere. It means being misunderstood, miscategorized, and misplaced. But I'm not the only one who was created as a mestizo. Jesus was a person between worlds long before I was. In his incarnate form, he too had a bicultural identity.

First, Jesus is both God and man. This is what we mean when we talk about the incarnation. Jesus steps outside of his original nature in heaven to become a man on earth. He is a celestial immigrant who leaves the realms of heaven to pitch his tent among men.

Second, he is born as a brown-skinned disenfranchised Jew in a Roman world. Matthew 2:13 clearly identifies Jesus as a refugee. The classic modern-day definition of a refugee is a person/family forced to flee their homeland for fear of persecution. This is exactly what happens to Jesus as a little boy, when Mary and Joseph flee to Egypt in order to save his life.

For much of his earthly life, Jesus experiences racial taunts and insults. One of his own disciples, Nathaniel, when he first hears of Jesus's origins, remarks, "Can anything good come from Nazareth?" (John 1:46a). After all, it *was* a poor and overlooked town. But God chooses Nazareth to be the hometown of our King.

In John 8, the religious leaders try to insult Jesus by calling him a demon and a Samaritan (a people group who were half-Jew and half-Gentile). At that time there was extreme racial tension between Jews and Samaritans. The leaders use the word

Samaritan as a racial slur—intended to shame Jesus's identity. But Jesus is not bothered by this taunt. Instead, these experiences propel his ministry forward.

Since Jesus is treated as a misfit and pushed to the margin, he also knows how to best love and care for others at the margins. He is an outsider himself and so he identifies especially with other outsiders. The same Jesus who is called a Samaritan is the One who goes out of his way to find and love a Samaritan (see John 4). The same Jesus who is called a demon is the One who heals the demon-possessed (see Luke 8). The same Jesus who is mocked for his hometown, seeks out his disciples from similar towns and villages. He doesn't visit the big cities or invite the wealthy, beautiful, or talented. Instead, Jesus seeks his disciples in Galilee, a rural region that was largely insignificant in the world's eyes, with a population of about 300,000 scattered in some two hundred villages. It's here that he first calls blue-collared fisherman to follow him.

You see, Jesus understood loneliness. He was rejected for many reasons, including the color of his skin and his ethnicity. Luke 9:58 tells us, "Foxes have holes and birds of the air have nests, but the Son of Man has nowhere to lay his head." Jesus knew how it felt to be misunderstood, to not ever feel at home in this world, and to be rejected. But for Jesus, all of these experiences were worth it. Despite the pain and the hardships he endured, he embraced being a misfit to meet us where we are. He acquired our customs, languages, and pains in order to care for us, to heal us, and to unite us. In fact, it is through his death and resurrection that Jesus embraced the way of suffering, the taunts, the pains of rejection, and even death so that we could be invited into his family among equals.

THE JESUS I WANT YOU TO KNOW

Maybe you are a misfit like me because of your skin color. Or maybe you're a misfit for other reasons. Whatever the case, or whatever you've been told, I want you to know that Jesus identifies with your feelings of isolation and misunderstanding; he was a misfit too. He knows your pain and identifies with your struggles. He welcomes you to come and share your heart and hurts with him.

Moreover, know that your experiences and feelings as a misfit can actually be a gift. It's the misfits who have a high radar for people on the margins. You know when someone is being bullied or shamed, because you've been there, and you also know how to empathize, care, and love on the hurting. This is how you can point people to Jesus.

Whatever it is that sets you apart, you have a powerful role to play in the kingdom of God. You are the bridge builders. Because you stand in the gap, you can fight for unity and reconciliation in a way that no one else can. As a mestizo—neither fully in one world or the other—you can be Christ's representatives to the world around you.

You are deeply loved by God. Rejoice and live in this freedom.

DEVOTIONAL QUESTIONS

Read Luke 8:26–38.

1. According to the text, how did the townspeople respond to this outsider—a wild man possessed by demons? How does Jesus respond to him?

2. The author of chapter 4 defines the word *mestizo* as a person in between worlds and never fully fitting in anywhere. It means being misunderstood, miscategorized, and misplaced. Have you ever felt like a mestizo?

3. The Bible affirms that Jesus loved mestizos—after all, he himself was one. How does this inform the way that you view and treat yourself, as well as others who are different, on the margins, or outsiders?

INCARNATION (noun): The event when God came down to earth and took on human flesh in the person of Jesus.

What this means for you: Because Jesus came to earth and experienced the pains of life, he can identify with your suffering. You can identify with him as a human being who was both hungry and thirsty, hot and cold. He suffered grief and sorrow and utter agony as he was crucified on the cross.

Chapter 5
Reputation and Righteousness
by Kristen Hatton

I had no business trying out for the cheerleading squad. I was a letterman on the soccer team with no prior cheerleading experience. But earning a spot on the squad was more about popularity, and less about skill.

For several weeks, I'd race from soccer practice to cheer practice. My soccer coach was furious. She couldn't comprehend why a rising senior would willingly abandon her starting position and leadership role for a place on the cheerleading squad. I had my reasons.

I envisioned myself at pep rallies and games, with all the underclassmen, including my freshman sister's friends, looking up to me. The only real obstacle (so I thought) in making the cut was the judges' approval at the prescreening tryout. My pride convinced me that the student body's vote would secure my spot.

Even when I couldn't master a back handspring, I rationalized that my spirit would make up for it. When the day finally arrived for pre-screening tryouts, I put on my ankle brace from a recent soccer injury, hoping it might earn some leniency from the judges. I reasoned that less precision would be expected from someone with an injury. I couldn't have been more wrong.

When the list of those who made the cut was posted, I raced to the school with other cheerleader hopefuls. As we crowded in on each other, trying to view the list, I began to panic.

Where is my name? I can't find it! Was it accidentally left off? Wishful thinking.

I had to face the difficult reality that I would not be a cheerleader. I tried covering my disappointment as I congratulated those standing by me whose names were on the list, including many of my good friends. Secretly, I was filled with envy. I didn't want to watch them cheering at football games, while I stood in the bleachers.

I began questioning God. Clearly the other girls weren't nearly as deserving as me. I rationalized my superiority—in popularity, school spirit, and outward actions. I was especially upset about one cheerleader in particular. She wasn't even a believer!

Why her and not me, God? I am the one living right. I should be the one who gets rewarded.

Until this point in time, I had considered myself an asset to God's kingdom. I assumed he was pretty thankful to have me on his team. After all, I brought a host of achievements. I went to church every Sunday, was involved with the youth group, Young Life, and Fellowship of Christian Athletes. I had my daily quiet time and even wrote a quiet time devotional for my youth group's weekly publication. On top of all that, I didn't drink or even go to parties. I was confused as to why God would not honor my obedience or want someone like me in a position of influence. Even more nonsensical to me was the fact he would give that status to a non-Christian party girl.

Oh, how foolish I was.

THE JESUS I WISH I KNEW IN HIGH SCHOOL

As I reflect back on the cheerleading incident, I realize that I was seeking my own glory and setting my hope there. I was completely unaware of the depth of my own sinfulness; I didn't even see my need for a Savior.

Now don't get me wrong—as a believer I identified as a sinner, but only in a generic sort of way. I viewed sin as outward behavior—and on the outside, I looked pretty good! I was careful to hide my ugly, inward desires like selfishness, pride, and my intense need for praise.

It's painful to peel away masks of perfection and performance and allow others to see me as I really am. Who I really was (and am) is sinful, selfish, and self-consumed. Who wants anyone to see *that*? But when my eyes saw sin as more than just behavior, I began to see my heart's true condition. I realized that I was no better than the cheerleader who earned *my* coveted spot. In fact, we were equal in the sense that we were both sinners deserving judgment and wrath. Thankfully, God extends grace to the guilty. And so he sent his Son.

I eventually learned that Jesus didn't come just to die for us. He came to *live* for us. And because he did, we've been given a better righteousness. You see, before Jesus could be our perfect sacrifice, he had to first accomplish living the perfect life required by God. For it was through his perfect living that he became the unblemished, sacrificial lamb.

Not only was Christ fully perfect and fully God, but he was also fully human. And it was in the fullness of his humanity that he never had a jealous thought. He never looked down on others or viewed himself as superior. He was never selfish with his time. He never snapped at his brother or disrespected his parents. He never secretly hoped someone else would mess up or look bad. He never sought revenge. He never sinned in any way, big or small, inwardly or outwardly.

Therefore, at the cross when Jesus took on all of our sin (past, present, and future), he exchanged it for his perfection. And it is his perfect righteousness that covers us completely, making us acceptable to God.

Practically, this means when pride continues to pop up in my life or when I manipulatively work to get my way, I am free to admit my selfish and sinful motives. I don't have to pretend it's not true, self-justify, or cover up. Instead, when I am confronted with my sin, I am free to seek forgiveness from God and others. I am also free from shame. I don't have to punish myself for my sin. Because Christ was perfect for me, God sees me as perfect. He is my righteousness.

As a teenager, I lived as if my good performance—my outward obedience and faith—earned God's blessings, like a position on the cheer squad. I looked down on others who failed to live up to *my* self-righteous standards (as if I were God but without any of his mercy). I failed to see my own sin.

Ironically, though I ascribed to the Christian belief that salvation comes by faith, I lived a works-based theology. This led to endless striving and the judgment of others. But the gospel I know now comes with surprising freedom. I now see myself as a sinner saved by grace. And because Jesus has freed me of my sin, I no longer need to hide, pretend, self-justify, or self-atone for my sin. I am free before God, and free to love others.

THE JESUS I WANT YOU TO KNOW

My hope is that you also will experience the freedom that comes in knowing, as Tim Keller said, "we're far worse than we ever imagined, and far more loved than we could ever dream."[1] We don't need to be perfect; Christ is perfect for us. We don't need to hide our sin; we are forgiven.

In Christ, you have a better righteousness than anything you could ever attain on your own. In Christ alone, you are fully and forever forgiven.

DEVOTIONAL QUESTIONS

Read Romans 3:23–24.

1. In this passage, the apostle Paul offers a solution to our fallen nature. What is it?

2. The author of chapter 5 describes her feelings of superiority to others, particularly the girl who took

---

1. Tim Keller, Twitter Post, February 15, 2015, https://twitter.com/timkellernyc/status/567005542770810880?lang=en.

her place on the cheerleading squad. Take a minute to consider your own sinfulness. Where are you in need of repentance?

3. We have all "fallen short" and are in need of a Savior. The grace given to us in Jesus allows us to both name our sin and also claim it forgiven. How can you live out this truth today?

JUSTIFICATION (noun): The two-fold process whereby a person's sins are forgiven and they, through faith, receive the perfect righteousness of Christ.

What this means for you: Because of Christ's perfect righteousness, you are now declared righteous and perfectly acceptable to God. As a result, you can feel comfortable in your own skin. There is nothing you can do to make yourself more or less worthy to God.

Chapter 6
Doubt and Love
by Mark Howard

I really loved Jesus in my youth. But I also experienced doubt—like the nagging feeling of guilt and fear that maybe, just maybe, he wasn't trustworthy. Would he *really* never leave me? Could his forgiveness *really* cover *all* my sin? Most of all, my relationship with Jesus often left me feeling worn out from trying so hard.

If you could have listened to my thoughts on any given day as a teen, you would have heard something like this:

"I'm so tired of trying to be good."

"Is this really worth it, or am I missing out on all the fun for nothing?"

"Will Jesus really give up on me if I _____?"

"Ugh, I'm so sorry! Please don't give up on me, Jesus! I'll try harder next time!"

"(Sigh) This better be worth it."

I'd be lying if I said these thoughts still don't creep back into my head from time to time. But now, after years of experiencing grace despite my insecurities, failures, and faults, my relationship with Jesus has deepened.

I have gotten to know a Jesus who is very much alive and at work in this world, who is unfailingly gracious, and whose patient presence simmers with loving-kindness.

But as a teenager, Jesus felt distant. Sure, there were moments during youth retreats or at Christian camp when I felt deeply connected to him—but those were the exception.

Back then, I knew Jesus as Lord, King, or Judge; I didn't know him as a friend.

I was vaguely aware that the word *Lord* had Jewish and Roman layers of meaning, but the only lords I knew about were British nobility. For me, a lord conjured up images of old men who were powerful and rich—but also standoffish, wrapped in wealth, and tinged with disdain for the commoner.

And that's how Jesus felt to me sometimes: a distant Lord with the privileged status of God's firstborn Son, and the treasure troves of heaven at his disposal. Sure, I could see how such a Jesus was worthy of praise and whose side you certainly wanted to be on. But I also worried that my rags would somehow offend his riches. When I was feeling insecure in my own skin, such thoughts kept me from drawing too close. They made me want to hide.

I remember sitting on the cold tile of the bathroom in my house with the door shut, feeling horrible about myself. I was ashamed and angry at my inability to get control of my thoughts. If Jesus really meant that even thinking about sex with a person was like committing adultery, then what hope did I have with my teenage hormones raging? I felt like dirt. I felt worthless. In those moments, the Lord Jesus felt safer from a distance.

As a teen, I viewed politicians as impersonal and out for themselves. They were preoccupied with their own agendas. While I knew Jesus wasn't a politician, I questioned if he was trustworthy. I didn't think he understood or cared about my personal struggles.

As a result, I really didn't expect much of Jesus. I inferred that my lot in life was largely up to me. While it seemed safe to acknowledge Jesus as Lord and King, I better get on with making the best of my own life.

Most often, and most exhausting, was my experience of Jesus as a judge, always watching and evaluating how I measured up.

Shortly after getting my driver's license, I had an experience that I can still feel in my bones today. I was behind the wheel and midway through crossing the train tracks near my house, when the lights on the crossbar started flashing. As soon as I got to the other side, a cop pulled out and turned on his siren.

My heart began to race and sweat broke out everywhere as I pulled to the side of the road. I knew I hadn't broken any laws, but I was a sixteen-year-old male with a new license. I was terrified. The cop had so much power over me, and from the look on his face, he knew it.

I understood that *how* I reacted could make a big difference in the outcome of this encounter. *Be polite. Be respectful. Be submissive. Don't argue.* Maybe he would be merciful.

After being threatened with a ticket, I only received a warning. And the warning worked—I still haven't gotten a ticket to this day!

As a teenager, a lot of my day-to-day relationship with Jesus felt like that experience with the police officer. I was painfully aware that I was at God's mercy. But my situation was worse than with the cop, because I knew that with Jesus I was guilty.

As a result, I was perpetually worried that Jesus would finally have enough, the "warnings" would run out, and I'd get a ticket—or worse. And so, like with the cop, I tried to do what I could to win Jesus to my side. I went to church. I played in the praise band. I got on the youth leadership team. I didn't do drugs. I didn't have sex. I wanted to do everything I could to earn his favor.

It was grueling, and I regularly wondered if it was worth it.

THE JESUS I WISH I KNEW IN HIGH SCHOOL

Over the last several decades, Jesus has patiently, wonderfully, and sometimes painfully worked in my life to shape my understanding of who he is and the nature of his affections for me.

A key turning point was coming to grips with the reality of the doctrine of adoption. Put simply, the doctrine of adoption believes that in Christ we become a part of God's family with all the benefits therein. It's why we get to call God, our Father.

What's truly remarkable, though, is that Scripture tells us that our adoption into God's family is not of secondary importance to our salvation. In fact, our adoption is a primary reason for Jesus's life, death, and resurrection.

Listen to what Paul writes in his letter to the Galatians: "When the fullness of time had come, God sent forth his Son, born of woman, born under the law, to redeem those who were under the law, *so that* we might receive adoption as sons" (4:4–5, emphasis mine).

So that.

Jesus came to redeem us *so that* we could become children of God. The good news is that Jesus doesn't just want our good behavior or righteousness. He wants *us* because he loves *us*, like a father loves his child.

The truth of our adoption changes everything—because while a king, lord, or judge might be distant and aloof, family is a different matter. Jesus wants to be near to us. He wants us to draw near to him. I'm an American, but I can't just run up to the President and expect to be embraced. If I did, the only open arms I would find would be those of the Secret Service—and it wouldn't be a loving, gentle embrace either. But nobody is going to stop one of the President's family members from getting a hug or seeking out attention.

I am far from a perfect father, but I know deep down that nothing could ever keep me from loving my children with everything I am. And if that's how I feel, how much deeper must God's love for his children be? "See what kind of love the Father has given to us, that we should be called children of God; and so we are" (1 John 3:1a).

And sure, I believe that God still watches me—but not as a mean-hearted judge wanting to exert his power over me with condemnation. Rather, Jesus sees me always through the lens of his unending love, always wrapped up in his own righteous robe. He watches over me as a mother delights in watching over her newborn child.

Because of this, I no longer feel insecure in God's love. "There is therefore now no condemnation for those who are in Christ Jesus," Paul writes in Romans 8:1. He goes on to say, "I am sure that neither death nor life, nor angels nor rulers, nor things present nor things to come, nor powers, nor height nor depth, nor anything else in all creation, will be able to separate us from the love of God in Christ Jesus our Lord" (vv. 38–39).

I wish I had known as a teenager the freedom of following Jesus happily as my Lord and King, simply because I knew he loved me and wanted me for his own. I wish I had felt free to draw near to Jesus, even in my sin. I now know that even my worst sin cannot outweigh his love for me.

THE JESUS I WANT YOU TO KNOW

My dear friend—I want you to know the Jesus who is always close, deeply gracious, and overwhelmed with love for you. If you feel far from him, unsure of whether following Jesus is worth it, and tired from trying to earn his favor like I was, please know you are not alone and that there is another way.

Draw near to Jesus. If you are unsure how, I would encourage you to find a quiet place alone. Turn off your phone. And then start talking to him. Ask him to show you that he is with you. Ask him to wrap you in his love like a mother or a father and to pour out his Spirit on you. Then, start sharing your heart as you would to the safest, closest friend you've ever had. Don't hold anything back. Once you have no more words, just sit, listen, and rest in him.

DEVOTIONAL QUESTIONS

Read 1 John 3:1.

1. The author of chapter 6 viewed God as Judge rather than Father. Have you ever seen God in this way?
2. Imagine the best parent in the world. What would they be like? How might your relationship with God change

if you saw yourself as a child of the most loving parent the world has ever known?

3. How might you pray differently now, knowing that God loves you as an adoring parent? Could you tell him anything and everything?

ADOPTION (noun): When a person puts their faith in Christ, they are adopted as a child of God. As his child, they receive all the benefits of being an heir of the King.

What this means for you: As an adopted child of the Most High God, you receive all the benefits of a child of God. You can draw close to him, as you would a loving parent. You can tell him everything. You are his.

Chapter 7
Dreams and the Real Story
by Charlotte Getz

As an adult, it's easy to block out the particular challenges of one's teenage years. Yet I was recently (a little painfully) taken back to my own high school struggles when I read the following passage from a Sally Rooney novel:

> Marianne had the sense that her real life was happening somewhere very far away, happening without her, and she didn't know if she would ever find out where it was and become part of it. She had that feeling in school often, but it wasn't accompanied by any specific images of what the real life might look or feel like. All she knew was that when it started, she wouldn't need to imagine it anymore.[1]

Marianne's inner experience as a teenager sounds awfully familiar to my own. I went to boarding school in Rhode Island for my last three years of high school and, although I had friends there, felt mostly unseen. I went about each day accompanied by the ever-present sense that I was not quite smart enough, not quite athletic enough, not quite pretty enough, a bit chubby, extremely colorful, and way *way* too loud; all at once too much,

1. Sally Rooney, *Normal People* (Richmond, UK: Hogarth, 2019), 11.

and yet not nearly enough. My role in this high school narra-
tive seemed to be playing out with all the grace of a sideshow
act—garish and uncomfortable to watch—rather than the cool
composure of a leading lady. I wondered why I was so very inca-
pable of walking a calmer, more neutral line of "normal" (whatever that meant).

For as long as I could remember I believed that a boyfriend,
a leading man, would be the solution to my angst. Having a
boyfriend starring opposite me would mean real and lasting
affirmation that I was somebody to be desired, somebody worth
loving, that my story was worth entering into, and that all my
awful suspicions about myself were in fact untrue. That I wasn't
just a kooky, average student who frequently got into trouble
for talking during class. Yet I continued to feel I was *all* of those
things and, evidently, also powerless to draw even a shred of
romantic attention from any of the (many) boys I liked.

This was not the wild, vibrant, magical story I'd dreamed
up for myself and my life when I was a child. No, I was lonely,
insecure, restless, and hungry for so much more than the disappointing, sometimes embarrassing plot unfolding before me.
During free periods, I'd lay in my dorm room bed and gaze out
a foggy window overlooking the school quad. I'd get lost in my
music and, like Marianne, achingly dream of the life I was missing—the thrilling, romantic, robust story that surely lay ahead,
if only I could write myself into it already.

Refrain as best you can from judgment, but I began to fan-
tasize about the future-Charlotte as a movie star. True story.
And not just your run-of-the-mill celebrity social media influ-
encer-type, but a well-respected Hollywood actress, the Oscar-
winning sort, like a young Meryl Streep. I imagined what it
would be like to have people take me seriously as I effortlessly
glided down red carpets (as opposed to the class clown reputation I'd acquired as a teenager). I imagined myself on the cover
of *People* magazine, my movies airing during prime time on
television sets across America, by now a household name the
likes of Sandra Bullock or Julia Roberts. If future-Charlotte

could be a movie star, that meant I'd finally be deemed "beautiful," which also meant I'd probably have the pick of the litter when it came to hunky boyfriends. "Movie Star-Me" would be known, seen, beloved: all the trimmings of a perfect, exciting, satisfying life story.

While I grew up in the church, I didn't know God or Jesus in any meaningful way until a few years into college. As a teenager, God seemed like some far-off entity who couldn't possibly understand my plight—much less have actually created me with divine purpose, meticulous intention, or abundant love. I half-heartedly asked him for things from time to time, as if he were a vending machine or some kind of mystical genie. But I lacked any firmer grasp of him than this vague figure in the sky who *might* grant my wishes if I begged hard enough. So instead of looking to God for my sense of identity and worth, I looked to other people, to boys, to my future adoring audiences as the measuring stick for who I should be and what my story should look like.

The story the world was laying out for me looked meager, incomplete, below average. I felt more invisible by the hour, as if a playwright had come to the not-so-painstaking conclusion to write insignificant-me straight out of his play: "This character is both too much, and not enough. Easier to just strike her from the script altogether."

THE JESUS I WISH I KNEW IN HIGH SCHOOL

I would learn a few years later that Christianity tells a different story than the world. Jeremiah 1:5 says this, "Before I formed you in the womb I knew you, and before you were born I consecrated you." What I wouldn't give to travel back in time and whisper these words into the ear of my high school self (although I suspect God was doing the job for me, all the while).

Jeremiah himself was a teenager when God called him to be a prophet to the nations. He was also deeply insecure, felt painfully inadequate: "I do not know how to speak, for I am only a youth" (Jeremiah 1:6b). And yet according to this verse, God had known Jeremiah, had set him apart, had chosen him for a purpose since the dawn of time. Can you imagine that the God of the universe knows you this intimately? That you, specifically, were in his heart and his mind since the very beginning?

In his book *Run with the Horses*, Eugene Peterson offers the following practical wisdom about this Scripture from Jeremiah:

> My identity does not begin when I begin to understand myself. There is something previous to what I think about myself, and it is what God thinks of me. . . . I never speak the first word. I never make the first move. Jeremiah's life didn't start with Jeremiah. Jeremiah's salvation didn't start with Jeremiah. Jeremiah's truth didn't start with Jeremiah. He entered the world in which the essential parts of his existence were already ancient history. So do we.[2]

This means that no matter how circumstances may appear, our lives are not an accident. Our identities are not what *we* make of them. Our stories are not failed spin-offs of a more impressive story. No, we were created with infinite love and purpose. Before the world was formed, we were written into *God's* story—this God who created the heavens and the earth, the winds and the rains, the daisies and the daffodils, and also our very inmost beings. This God who said to himself, "I want *Charlotte* in my story." And like a master craftsman, he knits us together in our mothers' wombs (see Psalm 139).

In all our anxieties and insecurities about who we are and what we're here for, God doesn't cheer for us off set like some motivational film director: "Find it in yourself! You have everything it takes!" No. When Jeremiah protests to God that he is only a child, God does not pat him on the back, coax him toward center stage and say, "Be your own hero, Jeremiah!" He says something far more inspirational: "Do not be afraid . . . for I am with you to deliver you" (Jeremiah 1:8). Then he touches

---

2. Eugene H. Peterson, *Run with the Horses: The Quest for Life at Its Best* (Westmont, IL: IVP Books, 2009), 37–38.

Jeremiah's mouth and says, "Behold, I have put my words in your mouth" (v. 9b). From the beginning to the end, God places the full weight of our enoughness—the arc and resolution of our characters—onto his own shoulders. He pours perfect strength into our weakness. As Jeremiah illustrates, he moves and saves, and we receive and respond. God created us to depend on him, and he is a far more worthy and capable provider than we could imagine. If you aren't convinced, look no further than the cross.

If you—like me—like Marianne—are waiting for your best self to take over, for your "real" life to start, for the better story to unfold, consider that the story you are in *right now* began centuries ago and it culminates with Jesus dying on a cross and three days later walking out of a tomb, *alive*. He did all of this on *your* behalf, because he has known you, dear reader, he has loved you from the very beginning.

The story I'd been longing for as a teenager only showed real sparks of magic once I understood my place in *God's* story. My immovable, irreplaceable role in the story of God was this: seen, loved, forgiven, known, *recipient*. You might notice that these are the very things I had sought from a boyfriend and from movie star-me. As a teenager I might have felt like a sideshow act, but to God I was a beloved leading lady worth dying for.

THE JESUS I WANT YOU TO KNOW

The God I know now says this to me and, filled in with different descriptors, *to you*: "I know exactly who you are. I created you and your story myself, like a script, writ with its very own font. I created you to be warm and friendly, maybe a little too loud and a little 'too much.' I created you to brim with wild and improbable dreams and also with the imagination to see some of them through. I created you to reveal my glory in a particular way. Just like Jeremiah, you are also 'not enough.' But I created you to need me; my strength, my rescue, *are* enough. I am with you. And I have set you apart. You can get out of your bed and stop *imagining* these things *could* be true, because they *are* true.

You are enough because of what I have done for you through Jesus. You are lovable because I love you, and I have proven that love to you in the most over-the-top, outlandish way possible—by laying down my very life for you."

DEVOTIONAL QUESTIONS

Read Jeremiah 1:4–10.

1. What is God's role in Jeremiah's story? How might this apply to your own story?
2. The author of chapter 7 describes longing for a more exciting story, a more extraordinary life. Can you relate? How?
3. Consider your life through the eyes of your Creator. How might he see it differently than you do?

IDENTITY IN CHRIST (noun): Who you are is based on who Christ is.

What this means for you: Christ has given you a clear identity in himself. Whether you are an athlete or musician, an artist or mathematician, the most important thing about you is this: You are sinful, but you are loved and rescued in Jesus Christ.

Chapter 8
Approval and God's Voice
by Sandra McCracken

I went on a Colorado ski trip with a friend's youth group in high school. I had been downhill skiing once a year or so with my family. I especially loved skiing with my dad and older brothers. They always took me out on the steeper passages, leaving me frozen and thrilled by the adventure.

On this weekend ski retreat, we attended Bible studies and meals offset by ample free time to ski. I met some new girls my age and we went out on the slopes, taking it easy on intermediate and green (beginner) runs. After lunch, as the sun was dipping down toward the horizon, we stopped for lunch and hot chocolate in one of the lodges on the top of the mountain.

While at the lodge, we met up with some older boys from the youth group. Feeling overly confident and chasing some attention from the boys, I parted ways with the girls I had met that morning, to ski with the guys on the harder slopes. I don't remember if anybody actually asked me to join, or if I just volunteered to tag along.

I wanted to prove I could keep up on the black (expert) slopes as I had occasionally done with my brothers. I wanted the affirmation that I was a good skier, that I could hang with the best of them. Growing up, I was always smaller than friends my age and I was often driven to prove that I could be as resilient, strong, and athletic as anyone. But it took effort to keep up this tough-girl charade. Inside, I was pretty tender. I spent energy trying to downplay my sensitive, artistic nature.

I traded out anything pink in my closet for black, oversized sweaters. I threw out bows and Barbies; I put off anything that would give away the little girl inside me that I was eager to leave behind. I wore soccer shoes and a camo jacket every day to school. I tried to build a shell of athleticism and bravery. But while trying hard not to appear weak or over-sensitive, I missed a chance to really be myself.

So, heading up the mountain on the first chair lift with this group of boys, I was determined to keep up. I hung in there for a while, but by the end of a long day my muscles were tired. We were finishing up by taking the route back to the base on some of the hardest slopes.

The last run down, everybody took off ahead of me.

I couldn't manage the steep incline, icy patches, and deeply cut moguls. As the rest of the crew descended further and further out of sight, I lost my courage and was stuck on the mountain.

The fear or fatigue took over, and I was scared to go on.

I carved wide, slow switchbacks, working perpendicular with the hill. But it ended up that the only way I could go somewhat down without going *straight* down was to go right into the woods. And once I was in the woods, I couldn't keep control. I veered off from the trail and got stuck in deep, powdery snow. I couldn't turn around and before too long, I couldn't see the way back.

The light started to fade in the sky and I began to worry that I might be stuck out there overnight. There were really only two directions I could go (other than straight down, which I couldn't do between the trees). I could either go through the woods across from where I started, hoping for an easier way down, or I could cut back to the difficult slope (which was a ways behind me now). I needed to pick one and stick with it.

This small lesson is one I've had to face many times when I've gotten myself into foolish situations like this one, when I couldn't go backward, but I didn't know the way forward: you just have to keep taking small steps in the same direction. Right or wrong, if you keep changing your mind, you'll end right where you started. Just. Keep. Walking.

I was lost in the woods. I stopped, started. Took off my skis. That didn't work. Put my skis back on. That didn't work either. I struggled for nearly an hour before realizing that the lifts had just closed. I cried and yelled with frustration.

But no one was around to hear me.

I was in over my ability, but in taking small strides in the same direction, I made my way slowly across the mountain cold, embarrassed, and scared. Through trees and over powder, I finally saw an opening through the other side of the trees.

In the clearing, I buckled my boots back into the skis' braces, wiggled my frozen toes, and skied the rest of the way down the mountain with tears of relief on my cheeks. The chair lifts were now closed, and the forest spit me out onto the far side of the mountain at a different base. So I threw my skis over my shoulder and walked to the bus stop where I waited for the next bus back to the lodge.

Back at the room, I pulled on dry clothes and socks and then I snuck in late for dinner.

I had been leading with my ego. I was chasing some attention or some thrill. I wanted to prove I was a good skier. But I ended up alone on the mountain, in the woods, in waist-deep snow on a steep incline. I was proud, trying to be cool, and it got me stuck.

THE JESUS I WISH I KNEW IN HIGH SCHOOL

In this episode of over-reaching and grasping for something I didn't need to prove, I missed out on real community, maybe even real friendships with the girls I had met that morning.

I still do these same kinds of foolish things sometimes. Thrill seeking, limit pushing. I think God has made us for adventure. And I think sometimes I need to realize that ringing a bell is not going to actually make me tougher or more impressive. When I lead with ego and ambition, I usually end up more alone. That's the irony. When I went seeking attention for prideful gain, I ended up on that mountain alone.

But what if we started with an understanding that God has already given us his full attention? "But God shows his love for us in that while we were still sinners, Christ died for us" (Romans 5:8). Before we went looking for him, before we had done a single thing to impress him, he came after us, literally coming down to earth to live with us. Not only that, but before he came to pursue us, we had run the other direction, followed our own trail, and rebelled against him in our selfishness. Even then, he set his love upon us and came to make us his own.

If this is our heartbeat, then it's a lot more fun when we are free to go have adventures. We've got nothing to prove, and nothing to lose.

Sara Groves has a song lyric that says this beautifully, "You will lose your confidence. In times of trial, your common sense. You may lose your innocence, but you cannot lose my love."[1]

The Jesus I wish I knew back then is the One who is both tender and strong. But, he's not strong because he has to prove his worth. He doesn't need to secure validation from anyone. Yet listen to the words of his Father: "You are my beloved Son; with you I am well pleased" (Luke 3:22b).

When I seek approval from others, I always come up short. But when I experience the approval that comes from Jesus, I am free to be myself and love others.

Have you ever considered that faith in Jesus means that the delight the Father has for Jesus is the very same delight he has in you? As you give your life to Jesus, through him, you also

---

1. Sara Groves, "You Cannot Lose My Love," *All Right Here* (Brentwood: Ino/Epic, 2005), saragroves.com.

can have the full acceptance, the full riches of life as a son or daughter of God.

You don't have to earn, or clamor, or get yourself lost in the woods trying to find God's acceptance.

Look at Jesus in the Scriptures. He doesn't use his power to try to make friends. He knows how much his Dad loves him, so he moves with ease in between tenderness and assertiveness.

He cries with his friends, like Mary and Martha. He gets angry with his friends sometimes, too. He always tells us the truth. He means what he says. He's focused on one thing: the approval of his Father, which he already has forever. The good life flows from there.

I now see when I look back that God made me in love—not for me to chase attention or hide my sensitivities. He has made me just the way that I am. "You search out my path and my lying down and are acquainted with all my ways" (Psalm 139:3).

In God's kindness to me over the years, I'm learning to hear that secure love from the Father. When I run off chasing some adventure, I miss out on God's love and get stuck in the woods. But God in his kindness is with us when we're lost. He brings us back to safety, guiding us to take slow, small steps in one direction.

THE JESUS I WANT YOU TO KNOW

The Jesus I want you to know is the One who takes your face in his hands when you're lost in the woods, the One who sees you there and brings you back home. It's not about what you do or don't do that causes him to love you. He already loves you for who you are. He has a plan for you, a hope and a future (see Jeremiah 29:11).

And in this moment as you read these words, God's Spirit is working in all the pieces of your life, even the ones that feel like they're fragmented and broken. He's not just putting the pieces back together, but he is reconciling all these things back to *himself*. "In him all things hold together" (Colossians 1:17b).

Whether you're racing down the mountain, or lost in the woods, listen for the approval of Jesus, listen for his voice over all the other voices. He is the one who holds you secure. He'll come and find you and bring you home to himself.

DEVOTIONAL QUESTIONS

Read Luke 3:22.

1. What does it mean that God is well-pleased with Jesus? What had Jesus done, at this point, to earn God's affection?
2. In chapter 8, the author describes trying to prove herself, and failing. Can you relate?
3. How would your life and ambitions transform if you listened to the voice of God above all others? *With you I am well-pleased.*

APPROVAL (noun): The belief that someone or something is good or acceptable.

What this means for you: You no longer have to tire yourself out seeking God's acceptance. Because of Christ's finished work on the cross, you already *have* the full approval of God himself—forever. He loves you. He delights in you. You are enough.

Chapter 9
Pride and Grace
by Watson Jones

My story begins on the South Side of Chicago during my high school years.

On January 5, 1999, I placed my faith in Christ. Up until then, I performed poorly in school and was an aspiring thug. I wasn't unique in this sentiment, because at that time my high school was well-known for gang activity. But everything changed upon my conversion. I was sold out to the Lord and vowed to give him my best forever.

This period of my life was one of great zeal. I was excited about Jesus and wanted everyone at school to be changed by the power of the gospel. I shared Christ every day. I started serving in my church's high school ministry and later that same year, I sensed a call to preach.

It was then that something dark surfaced within me—an arrogance and pride. I had no room for grace. This mindset played out in two ways: first in my relationship with God. I assumed any goodness he sent my way was because of my own spiritual fervor and performance. It also played out in how I engaged with my peers. Because I didn't use profane language anymore, I judged anyone else who did. When I felt strong in my faith, I judged those who appeared weak. Anyone who wasn't on my level of spirituality, perfection, or intellect were immediately deemed inferior.

As long as I could perform, I was all good. But my arrogance could only conceal my personal deficiencies for so long.

As a young, judgmental, and arrogant preacher, I didn't have many friends and often felt lonely. In time, my passion began to wane, and I questioned my salvation. I wondered if God was even pleased with me. Furthermore, I was consumed with lust. Sex was *always* on my mind. My personal doubts, loneliness, and desire for sex made me wonder: "Does God even love me?"

All of these things converged during my senior year of high school. On September 11, 2001, I watched on television as the Twin Towers of the World Trade Center crumbled to the ground. And in that moment, I realized my faith was crumbling, too. I believed I was no longer good enough for God, so I decided to quit ministry.

My heart grew cold toward the Lord. I wanted to enjoy my senior year doing whatever I wanted, living life with no consequences. Suddenly I became all the things I used to judge in others. Profanity flowed from my mouth like water from an open faucet. My chief aim, aside from securing a place in college, was to have sex. Deep down I felt lost, ashamed, and discouraged.

When I entered my freshman year of college, my faith was on life-support. But God used a professor to bring me back. As one who has always been intrigued by history, I decided to schedule a meeting with Dr. Bradley Gundlach. What began as a single conversation around Roman history and culture moved to a weekly meeting that lasted the duration of the school year. He was a godsend for me. Together we did a Bible study through the book of Romans. It was then that I learned how to walk by grace.

THE JESUS I WISH I KNEW IN HIGH SCHOOL

While James 1:13 is clear that God does not tempt anyone toward evil, in retrospect, the Lord used my failings to utterly humble me and to teach me a lesson about grace.

The crux of my issue was my tendency toward performance. But who could blame me? As a child, I was ranked by how well I performed in class, not on the inherent value of my personhood. We live in a merit-based society where we are all measured by how well we perform. The world is just that cruel because there are no handouts. You are measured by what you produce. The more you produce, the "better" or more valuable you are deemed. This breeds a sense of arrogance in high performers, and I was no exception.

The problem exists when we carry this performance-based mindset into our relationship with God. It is very easy to believe God's love for us is rooted in what we bring to the table. When we feel we are serving God enough or being the best Christian, we become arrogant. But when we fall, we experience shame, guilt, and despair.

The gospel is the cure for our performance-based arrogance, and it is the balm to our brokenness. This is what I wish I knew as a teenager.

In the city of Dubai in the United Arab Emirates stands the Burj Khalifa, the tallest skyscraper in the world, at 2,722 feet tall. Consider this: our sins mount higher than Burj Khalifa, and God sees each and every one of them. But here's the good news: he offers us full forgiveness when we trust in his Son.

In Romans chapters 3–5, the apostle Paul discusses the idea of justification by faith. To be justified means to be acquitted, or to have your transgressions (sins) cleared. It is a legal idea where God, who is the Judge, declares us innocent of crimes that we have committed. Along with the acquittal of guilt, we begin a new relationship with God.

Jesus "was delivered up for our trespasses and raised for our justification" (Romans 4:25). This reality only happens by faith in Jesus's finished work on the cross. This justifies us, declares us innocent, and connects us with God forever. It is not the result of our performance, but rather of *Jesus's* performance for us.

Hear the beauty of Paul's words in Romans 5:1–2: "Therefore, since we have been justified by faith, we have peace with God through our Lord Jesus Christ. Through him we have also obtained access by faith into this grace in which we stand, and we rejoice in hope of the glory of God." That, friends, is grace.

We don't have to prove to God or ourselves that we are good enough. Paul says in Ephesians that salvation is a gift, "not your own doing; it is the gift of God" (Ephesians 2:8b). The free gift of God's acceptance eliminates our need to perform. We can now live in freedom, with grace for ourselves and others. We are free to serve the Lord knowing that his love lasts forever.

The day I realized this in the Bible study with Dr. Gundlach, I was changed. While I am grateful for the lesson, I wish I'd known this in high school. It would have saved me much heartache and despair.

THE JESUS I WANT YOU TO KNOW

What does all of this have to do with you? I'd be right to tell you that God opposes the proud, or that the haughty are always brought down. You'd be right to hear it and obey the Lord on the matter. I could tell you that you matter to God and you'd be right to believe that too.

But I want to speak to the deeper motives of the heart. A lot of times we are proud and arrogant because we feel the need to prove ourselves to God and to ourselves.

Grace takes that off of the table.

It doesn't matter what you've done. It doesn't matter how broken you feel. You do not have to bear the burden of your own performance. God's love for you is immense and he demonstrates it through the death of his only Son Jesus. Therefore, you can never be good enough to gain more love and acceptance; you can never be bad enough to lose it.

Walk in the freedom that grace affords.

DEVOTIONAL QUESTIONS

Read Romans 5:1–2.

1. How does being justified by faith free you from the need to prove yourself and your worth?

2. How can you identify with trying to prove yourself by performance, either in your spiritual life or in things like school, sports, music, etc.?

3. How do you think it would feel to trust that Christ has truly made you worthy? What words would you use to describe it?

GRACE (noun): God's underserved love and favor for sinners through Christ.

What this means for you: If salvation was determined or based on your good deeds or moral behavior, you'd be out of luck. The truth is, you are a sinner like everyone else. But God in his incredible grace does not tire of forgiving or rescuing his children.

Chapter 10
Sin and Rest
by Dawson Cooper

I remember telling my parents I could handle it. While sitting alone in my freshman dorm room, I told them I'd pull myself up by my bootstraps. I'd get the train back on its tracks. I'd be strong and navigate my unplanned pregnancy at eighteen years old.

What I found over the next nine months was that I could not handle it, nor could I fix it.

My entire high school career had been relatively smooth sailing. I had wonderful friends, was involved in various leadership positions, and had dated the same boy since the ninth grade. I was a Christian, involved in church and youth group. I didn't give my parents trouble and made good grades. I was accepted early to my dream college. All had gone as planned.

Yet I was the girl staring at a positive pregnancy test at eighteen years old, a few weeks into my freshman year of college.

The coming days were not easy. My boyfriend and I had to make life-changing, life-affirming, and life-demanding choices that would affect not only us but our unborn baby. Telling families and friends that I was pregnant, and would soon be married, feels surreal to me even now.

Can you imagine systematically calling a list of people to tell them how you made a mistake, a very personal one at that? Think of a struggle in your own life—one you'd rather keep private. Now imagine telling your parents and friends that you succumbed to it.

I found myself in that very position—exposed, ashamed, and guilty.

At the same time, I was intent on being strong. I would do what I needed to: tell people, plan a wedding, and go to the doctor. I assumed that if I did all the right things, people wouldn't see my brokenness, weakness, and sin. They'd see me holding it all together.

My husband and I married and completed the final exams of our first semester in college. Then we packed up my dorm room and moved to an apartment near his college, all before Christmas break.

Despite the support from family and friends, our situation was isolating. Transferring from my dream college was hard for me; watching friends hang out in a dorm while I went to doctor's appointments was disorienting; learning how to be married while everyone else was going to sorority swaps was lonely.

But acknowledging the pain in my heart would only expose my weakness, and that was best kept unseen. I could let go of my old life. I could move on. I was strong. I was back on track—a different track, but a track.

Yet that summer, as I sat at the lake holding our six-week-old son, I remained broken.

We had a precious, healthy baby boy, and our marriage was stable and happy. However, guilt and shame were two sidekicks I could not escape. No measure of strength, maturity, or just moving on could ever erase my shame and guilt.

THE JESUS I WISH I KNEW IN HIGH SCHOOL

On that day at the lake, I was reading my Bible and came across Matthew 11:28–30, which says, "Come to me, all who labor and are heavy laden, and I will give you rest. Take my yoke upon you, and learn from me, for I am gentle and lowly in heart, and you will find rest for your souls. For my yoke is easy, and my burden is light."

It sunk in as I read that verse how tired I was of carrying the guilt of my own sin, of disappointing others, of not being able to live up to the expectations of myself and others. I couldn't be strong. I couldn't fix what was done. I was not a perfect teenager, college student, daughter, or mom. And I couldn't try to chase the illusion of perfection anymore. I was flat-out exhausted from trying.

This verse from Matthew felt like water in a desert to me. It felt like a weight being lifted off my back. When I confessed my striving and self-sufficiency—and turned over the burden of my sin—I experienced unfathomable rest. I felt like I had finally found an answer to my shame and guilt, and it was in Jesus.

I realized that there was another side to the God I thought I knew.

I never realized how deeply I needed Jesus.

Jesus tells the Pharisees, who looked like they had it all together, "Those who are well have no need of a physician, but those who are sick. I came not to call the righteous, but sinners" (Mark 2:17).

In high school, I did not know the depth of my sin until my sin was exposed. I did not know my need for Christ's healing until I came to the end of myself.

Jesus, the Son of God, came to rescue his beloved people. And if someone is getting rescued, it is because they actually need rescuing. You don't sort-of-need-help when you are drowning. You need rescue! Because we are all naturally drowning in sin, we need Someone to get the lifeboat and pull us out of the water.

No matter how good I appeared on the outside, I was desperate for rescue.

Through Jesus's death on the cross, God does just that. Jesus, our Savior, took on the punishment for our sins—past, present, and future. John 3:16–17 says, "For God so loved the world, that he gave his only Son, that whoever believes in him should not perish but have eternal life. For God did not send his Son into the world to condemn the world, but in order that the world might be saved through him."

Our sin is expunged from our record because Jesus lived the perfect life for us, and died the death of a sinner for us. Even more so, Jesus defeated sin and death when he rose from the grave. God now looks on us as he looks on Jesus. Our relationship with God is restored to the point that "there is therefore now no condemnation for those who are in Christ Jesus" (Romans 8:1).

The more I saw my sin, the more precious and dear the cross became to me. I needed Jesus to save me. I needed God's forgiveness because I was imperfect. But more than that, I saw the person of Jesus as tender and patient, offering undeserved favor to a sinner like me. He came to save me, not to condemn me to a life of guilt and shame.

Drowning in my sin was horrible. It was tiresome and exhausting. Yet, had I not become pregnant at eighteen, I might not have received a greater understanding of who Jesus is, of what the gospel is, and why I need it.

Despite how hard that season was, I look back on it gratefully. I didn't have to wait until I was twenty-five or fifty to understand my inability to save myself. Not only did I gain a precious child (and husband), but I gained Jesus in a most necessary and transformative way. When I look back on those months of my pregnancy and early motherhood, I see Jesus's fingerprints throughout. He never left me, even when I didn't know I needed him. And when I saw my need for him, he opened his arms without condemnation. He didn't ask what took me so long, or why I couldn't have done everything right.

Jesus not only saved me, but he gave me freedom and life in a way that I could not have imagined as an incoming college freshman.

THE JESUS I WANT YOU TO KNOW

God already knows your sin, but you need his light to see it. Ask God for help to see your sin and need. Trust that what Satan uses for evil, God uses for good. God will find a way to use your sin to reveal your desperate need of him.

Friend, Jesus calls the sick, and that includes you. When you feel weak, tired, and broken, come to Jesus. He doesn't tell you to buck up and be stronger. He doesn't condemn you to a life of shame and guilt. Instead, he takes the burden and pain of sin and heals you. In that forgiveness and healing comes rest. Rest from your striving to be perfect. Rest from the pressure to keep it all together. Rest for the weary and broken. Come to Jesus and be healed—his yoke is easy, his burden light.

DEVOTIONAL QUESTIONS

Read Matthew 11:28–30.

1. How does Jesus describe himself? How does that description compare with your burdens? Which seems like the lighter load?

2. The author of chapter 10 describes wrestling with sin and shame. When have you felt "weary and heavy laden" with your sin?

3. The author allows her shame to lead her to Jesus. Because of her circumstances, she finally understood her need of him. Are you aware of your need for Christ? How might it feel to hand your burdens over to him?

SIN (noun):
1) Disobeying God's commands (behavioral)
2) Desiring to be the god of your own life (theological)
3) Separation from God (relational)

What this means for you: If you carefully and honestly look at your life, the magnitude of your sin should be clear. But because of Jesus, your sin is no longer counted against you. The more aware you are of your failures and shortcomings, the more you can rely on Christ's salvation.

Chapter 11
Failure and a Sure Promise
by Sam Bush

I started going to a new school in fifth grade. As exciting as it was to be in a new place—new classmates, new teachers—I didn't have anything or anyone to cling to. Every person in the world is hardwired for a sense of belonging and connection. So how was I going to fit in? How could I get people to like me?

I convinced myself that in order to belong, I had to be special. I wasn't the funniest, most athletic, or most talented; that was obvious. So I turned to schoolwork. That was going to be my key to success.

My first semester, I worked hard. *Really* hard. I wanted to prove myself. I wanted to make a good first impression. I wanted people to think I was smart. At first, it worked. At the end of the semester, awards were given out according to your grades and I got the highest award: First Honors *with Distinction*. Truth be told, I didn't even know what the word *distinction* meant, but I knew that it meant I was special.

At the end of the second semester, the same award ceremony took place and I was given First Honors (but *without* Distinction). The following year, I was given Second Honors, and so the downward trajectory continued. Despite my best efforts, First

Honors with Distinction was a one-time achievement. I never tasted the sweet victory of being distinguished again.

A favorite jazz trumpet player (and former professor of mine), John D'earth, once said, "You're only as good as your last solo." The trouble with my life is that my "solo"—which was my academic success—kept getting worse and worse. Rather than climbing the ladder of success, I felt like I was on the descent.

As I got older, school became more difficult. It would take me twice as long to read a book as some of my other classmates. No matter how hard I worked, a lot of the material just didn't come as naturally to me as it did for my classmates.

To cover my lack of intelligence, I posed as the quiet genius in the corner, the kid who rarely spoke, but, whenever he *did* say something, would offer some prophetic mic drop. Something like, "It's pretty obvious that *The Old Man and the Sea* is really about humanity's collective struggle with how we're all going to die." (Boom! Right?) And yet, too much of my reputation was riding on these one-line performances. What if my words weren't wise enough to deem me special? What if I was actually completely wrong about *The Old Man and the Sea*? I was trying to project the persona of a wise sage, but, as time wore on, I would rarely ever speak. Better to be silent than wrong.

I eventually became too self-conscious to say anything at all. Ironically, schoolwork, that which was going to distinguish me from everyone else, led to me becoming completely indistinguishable.

By the time I graduated high school, it was clear that I was *not* distinguished.

During my first semester of college, I nearly failed Economics. No matter how hard I tried—and I hate to admit that I actually tried really hard—the material was not connecting. I was mortified. Years ago, I was a straight-A superstar, and now I was barely passing entry level classes. What happened? How did I lose my scholarly mojo so completely? Was I on a downward spiral of failure? Who was I if I wasn't smart? Was life only going to keep getting worse?

THE JESUS I WISH I KNEW IN HIGH SCHOOL

The world measures us by what we do. Our accomplishments, our failures, these are what define us. The gospel, on the other hand, tells a different story.

I wish I had known as a teenager that the gospel highlights what *God* has done, rather than what *you* have done. Because of Jesus's work on the cross, God sees you as his beloved child.

The day before my final exam in Economics, while having lunch with my college minister, I began to grasp the truth of the gospel. I confessed, "I'm trying so hard in this class, but I just know I'm going to fail, and there's nothing I can do about it." I was spent. I had tried my best and I had failed (or was about to).

He calmly looked at me and said, "I know you probably can't believe this right now, but it's okay. I'm not just saying that. It's actually okay."

His message was direct and sincere. He wasn't puffing me up with pity or false assurance. He didn't try to boost my confidence by saying that I was actually very smart and would ace the test. He took my anxiety seriously. He faced it straight on without flinching. Rather than trying to quell my emotions, he listened to me (for quite a long time, actually), and he responded with truth and grace. Did I believe his words—that everything would be okay? Absolutely not. But I can see now that he was right.

In the end, I did fail (although the grading curve raised my test score to a 60%, so I did, technically, pass the course). My worst nightmare, in a sense, had come true. But by the grace of God, it really was okay. I might not have felt that completely at the time, but twenty years later I can say with confidence, it was okay. Despite our failures, despite our sins, despite our fear, God has made all things right. This is what the apostle Paul was talking about when he wrote, "And we know that for those who love God all things work together for good, for those who are called according to his purpose" (Romans 8:28).

When all else has failed (or when we literally *fail* in life) one thing remains: God's promise. Much to my dismay, I am more prone to hear God's faithful promise *after* I have failed.

It is only *in* my failure when I begin to recognize my need for a Savior. Strangely enough, Jesus's death on the cross—which accomplished our salvation—looked like a total failure. As he hung in shame, mocked and rejected, Jesus was lovingly righting every wrong. What appeared to be weakness was strength. What appeared to be the end was the beginning. He was victorious over all sin and death—all fear and failure.

Do I actually believe this? Most of the time, I do not. To be honest, I still worry a lot about the future. I still think if I fail, I will be doomed. Thanks be to God, the gospel is true no matter what I feel. Through Jesus's work on the cross, I am forever made right in him.

Jesus takes your sins and fears seriously. So seriously, in fact, that he died to repair the damage you have caused. He took all your sin and failure with him to the grave and rose again victorious, so that you might now live in truth and grace.

Imagine it this way: one day you're approaching the throne of God and he opens a very large book and it says [Your Name] and, "A Biography, Complete with Thoughts, Words and Deeds." The margins are filled with all the things that you didn't do. And God reads it. There's good stuff in there: all of your accomplishments and good deeds; there's that time you helped a homeless person; when you went out of your way to help a stranger. There's also that time when you gossiped about your friend. When God gets to the end of the book, no matter who you are or what you've done, the final verdict will end with one word: *unrighteous*. No matter how hard you worked in life, that is your final grade.

But imagine a different scene. God pulls out a book that is, in comparison to the first one, very small. It begins with, "He was born among the animals in a town called Bethlehem . . ." and ends with, "You are my beloved Son."

In other words, your biography is not the basis of your righteousness. Jesus's birth, life, and death have taken the place of your birth, life, and death. If you want to learn more about this great exchange, check out the Gospels: Matthew, Mark, Luke, and John. Through Christ, your identity begins and ends with

Jesus. It began in a manger. It was established on a cross, and it was fulfilled in his resurrection.

THE JESUS I WANT YOU TO KNOW

I'm not going to expect you to believe what I couldn't believe when I was younger. I still have a hard time believing that everything will be okay! But, by God's grace, I aim to trust the cross of Christ where God made everything right.

No matter what you are going through right now, dear reader, I firmly believe that God will make it right. He is with you this very moment and takes your worries seriously. If you are striving and failing, you can trust that God has won the battle on your behalf. His righteousness is your covering. As the great hymn "In Christ Alone" proclaims: "My Comforter, my All in All, Here in the love of Christ I stand."[1]

DEVOTIONAL QUESTIONS

Read Romans 8:28.

1. How might this verse encourage you?
2. The author of chapter 11 shares hope for anxiety and doubt. Where do you need hope?
3. Where have you failed in life? How might dwelling on the gospel shape your response to failure?

---

1. Stuart Townend and Keith Getty, "In Christ Alone," *Lord of Every Heart* (Brentwood: Thankyou Music, 2001), Gettymusic.com.

HUMAN BEING VS. HUMAN DOING (nouns):
Many people believe that their worth is found in *doing* (actions and achievements). But, worth is actually found in *being* created in God's image, formed by his love.

What this means for you: Because of Jesus, you no longer have to earn your place in this world. You can take a deep breath, and give thanks to God. Everything that needs "doing" has already been done on the cross.

Chapter 12
Heartbreak and God's Presence
by Catherine Allen

As I let you in on my high school stories, I have to admit that it feels more like a confession than anything else.

Imagine driving around in your car, blaring music and analyzing texts between you and your crush. Every day to and from school, my friend and I would discuss the latest updates on the boys in our lives. While the carpool ride was very short, we could unpack a lot of information. My little white sedan was a sacred space that held all my secrets. We would get in the car each afternoon and immediately share what had happened that day. The daily report was filled with all exchanges made: texts, hallway interactions, glances, Facebook messages, weekend plans, dreams, and hopes for tomorrow.

One of the first things that comes to mind when I think of high school is boys and romance. And what comes to mind when I think of romance is sweaty hands. Not just clammy, but full-on *sweaty*. The perspiration on my palms was an outward projection of an inward problem. I was anxious and eager to have a boyfriend. I want to blame growing up with a soundtrack of Taylor Swift as the reason for my deep-seated romantic side, but the problem was this: my desire to be loved was infinitely greater than my desire to love.

When I look back at my high school years and my desire for romance, every cliche comes to my mind. However, the one that was stamped on my heart had to be: "It will happen when you least expect it." Believing this to be true, I would convince myself that if I tried not to expect it, then things would definitely work out in my favor. I remember one of my youth leaders sharing that she had her first kiss at twenty-two. I scoffed—certain I'd have had several boyfriends by then—maybe even be engaged!

As a teenager, there was not a single day when I did not hope for a boyfriend. And while the majority of my friends had boyfriends throughout those years, I did not end up dating anybody. Moreover, I went to a Homecoming dance only once out of all three years of high school, and I was not asked to prom my senior year.

While never being asked or chosen in high school definitely made me feel insecure, unwanted, and unlovable, nothing was quite as painful as unrequited affection. Obviously, I always noticed the cute boys and gossiped about them with my friends. However, my biggest crush was on the same boy for about four years. He and I had one million classes together and ran in the same friend group. He was sarcastic, and I adored him. He would zoom past me in his silver BMW, and I was elated. Guaranteed to see him Monday through Friday during Latin and History classes, my nerves were especially heightened. To manage my fears (and my sweaty palms), I tried to control my expectations, my looks, the way I was perceived, my intelligence, my social life, etc. I thought that if I was better at controlling these things, then I would be more desirable. Day after day, I would wonder what and when something would happen between us.

Three years into this very long and very one-sided crush, I received a text from his best friend that read something to the tune of, *he would never ever be interested in me.* Filled with heartbreak, rejection, and sadness, my crush and I met up over ice cream where he apologized for his friend's tough-to-swallow words. In my heart, I secretly hoped that he would say his friend was mistaken and he actually wanted to be with me. Instead, I just left with embarrassment and shame.

The heartbreak did not end there. Several years later, I entered into my first serious relationship. The closing line of our breakup went something like this: *I had some good features, but in the end he wasn't sure the good outweighed the bad*. In high school, these words would have crushed me. And while they certainly stung, by the grace of God I had an awakening in that moment: I had never felt more confident that those words were the opposite of God's love for me.

Although I heard the good news of the gospel, the proclamation of God's unshakable love did not resonate with me until after high school. Sadly, deep down, I believed I wasn't good enough. I also believed that if I made enough modifications to myself, I would secure a boyfriend. As a chubby, outgoing, unathletic, mediocre student, I believed that if I was smarter, more attractive, and more soft-spoken, I would be desirable. After confiding in a mentor about my fear of being single forever, she gently reminded me that "there are no leagues in souls." While we tend to measure someone as "in" or "out" of our league, she wanted me to hear that our worth is incalculable in God's kingdom because we are all sinners, immeasurably loved by an even greater Savior. I was desperate to hear it, but still did not quite believe it.

THE JESUS I WISH I KNEW IN HIGH SCHOOL

Sally Lloyd-Jones in *The Jesus Storybook Bible* says, "It's not about keeping rules! . . . You don't have to be good at being good for God to love you. You just have to believe what Jesus has done and follow him. Because it's not about trying, it's about trusting."[1] This message of grace continues to cover me. It soothes my wounds with each announcement: *you are loved as you are*.

---

1. Sally Lloyd-Jones, *The Jesus Storybook Bible: Every Story Whispers His Name* (Grand Rapids: ZonderKidz, 2007), 340.

My constant striving to be loved was best met in Christ, my Savior. He is the One who leaves the ninety-nine to find the one (see Luke 15:3–7). He is the One who seeks and saves sinners. He is the One who is filled with delight—bursting with celebration—at the rescue of one soul. "And when he found it, he lays [us] on his shoulders, rejoicing. And when he comes home, he calls together his friends and his neighbors, saying to them, 'Rejoice with me, for I have found my sheep that was lost'" (vv. 5–6).

There is nothing that can keep God at arm's length, because he is always rejoicing over you and he promises that he will never leave you (see Hebrews 13:5). Your "bad" thoughts, words, and deeds are no secret to Jesus. Psalm 139:4 says, "Even before a word is on my tongue, behold, O Lord you know it altogether." Not only does he know it, but his love bears it, endures it, and continues to the end (see 1 Corinthians 13).

In adolescence, I missed the true Lover—the One who welcomes me with full love and acceptance. I viewed God solely as a cheerleader—someone there to spotlight my accomplishments and encourage me to "victory." However, what I know now is that the victory was already won, boyfriend or not. I didn't need to be more or less of anything to earn the love of Jesus—I always had it.

Brennan Manning says it best in *Abba's Child*:

> We cannot assume that [God] feels about us the way we feel about ourselves—unless we love ourselves compassionately, intensely, and freely. In human form Jesus revealed to us what God is like. He exposed our projections for the idolatry they are and gave us the way to become free of them. It takes a profound conversion to accept that God is relentlessly tender and compassionate towards us just as we are—not in spite of our sins and faults (that would not be total acceptance), but with

them. Though God does not condone or sanction evil, He does not withhold his love because there is evil in us.[2]

THE JESUS I WANT YOU TO KNOW

While it may feel like God is far because you lost the perfect crush or feel unworthy, he is near to the broken-hearted and saves the crushed in spirit (see Psalm 34:18). Like me at times, the heartbreak and rejection might make you feel like the least of these, but God's grace is still abundant (see Ephesians 2:8).

My hope is that while worldly love might be hard to come by, you will trust God's steady, constant, faithful love, for it will endure forever. The good and the bad does not hold the power to change what Sally Lloyd-Jones calls, "the Never Stopping, Never Giving Up, Unbreaking, Always and Forever Love of God he showed us in Jesus!"[3] (how romantic is that?). He doesn't love you because you've crafted the perfect, witty prayer. His love does not hinge on what you look like, what you say, what you're interested in, or who you're friends with. God does not love you because he is obligated. He sees you fully, freely, and forever.

DEVOTIONAL QUESTIONS

Read Luke 15:1–7.

1. How does this passage express Jesus's love and pursuit of his people?
2. The author of chapter 12 discusses a love without conditions. Consider some examples of love you have received in life: both conditional and unconditional.
3. How does God's unconditional, eternal love encourage your heart?

---

2. Brennan Manning, *Abba's Child: The Cry of the Heart for Intimate Belonging* (Carol Stream, IL: NavPress, 2015), 3.
3. Lloyd-Jones, *The Jesus Storybook Bible*, 340.

IDOLATRY (noun): Ascribing value to things of this world that should actually be assigned to God himself. Examples might include viewing money, success, or popularity as equal to God.

What this means for you: As a sinner, you naturally make good things into idols. Understanding that only God can satisfy and save you—not a college acceptance letter, or a boyfriend, or a place on the team—leads you to rightly seek your joy and fulfillment in God.

Chapter 13
Morality and God's Gift
by Jessica Thompson

Our family was the superhero Christian family. Everyone was either a pastor, a missionary, or a Sunday school teacher. Everyone was always doing the most for God. Each time the church doors were opened, our family was there. Sunday morning, Sunday night, Wednesday evening, we spent more time at church than we spent anywhere else besides school and home. If the pastor needed someone to come and clean the bathrooms, my parents would volunteer us to do it. Truly, church was like our second home.

I learned really early on that the best way to make everyone happy was to play the "good Christian girl," and I did it with everything in me. When I was in kindergarten, I won "Ms. Christian Character"—the award given to the five-year-old who acted the most like a Christian, or told on the most kids for not acting like a Christian. I am not sure which characteristic won me the award, but I am sure I did both with excellence. So from kindergarten on, everything I did was in effort to uphold the idea that I was the kind of girl you wanted your kids to be friends with, because I would make sure that we were all doing the right thing *all the time*.

I was committed to this charade of following the rules so that I would think well of myself and have others think well of me. I loved hearing all the adults tell me how "good" I was. I really thought that if I could just be good enough, God would love me more and my parents and grandparents would love me more and then I would be happy.

This line of thinking led to everything but happiness. I was often sad that I still didn't quite measure up, and then sometimes I was angry with others because they weren't following the rules the way I thought they should. It was a confusing time for me.

As a high schooler, I continued to play the part of the upright, rule-following Christian. I went on short-term mission trips during the summer, I had a Bible verse stitched onto my letterman's jacket, and I was always the one talking about God and inviting people to youth group. While at youth group, I was the kid who sat up front. I felt like it was my job to make the youth pastor's job easy. I wanted to be the trophy kid of the group. Similar to when I was younger, this behavior worked for me in several different ways. First, everyone seemed happy with me. Second, it kept everyone out of my life because they all thought I was doing great.

The truth is, behind the scenes I was constantly trying to gain love and acceptance by attempting to make boys want me. I was constantly lying. I cheated on my boyfriend and tried to get with my close friends' boyfriends. My life was one big tangled ball of deception.

I went to Bible college right out of high school to get my bachelor's degree in theology—I wanted to study God and the Bible, but not because I loved God or the Bible. I loved following the rules; I loved approving of myself; I loved having others approve of me; I loved the sense of control that rule-following gave to me. I loved feeling superior to everyone else who wasn't following the rules. But I didn't *love* God. God seemed harsh and demanding. I mean who else would create rules that took away all the fun—and then expect me to live by those rules?

I was willing to keep the fake me, the good-me image, going for as long as I needed. But God had different plans.

One of the requirements for Bible college was that you had to attend a prayer service before classes started. I would typically use that time to snooze in my chair. If we had smart phones back then, I would have for sure been on social media or scrolling through memes. I remember very specifically that during one of my nap times, God interrupted me and both literally and spiritually woke me up. In that moment, God broke into my mundane thoughts and apathy and almost in an instant changed my mind and showed me a better way.

I'm not really sure how to explain what actually happened except to say that he impressed on my heart that all of my goodness, all of the good things that I tried to do, all the rules I tried to follow wouldn't make me right with him. I needed the work of Jesus in my life to truly make me good or, as the church people like to say, I needed the work of Jesus—not my own work—to make me holy and righteous. I realized that it wasn't all up to me to pull it off anymore. I realized that someone saw me exactly as I was, my truest self, and chose to love me anyway.

THE JESUS I WISH I KNEW IN HIGH SCHOOL

I think that sometimes, without realizing it, the church or the leaders in the church put too much emphasis on "doing big things for God," or "being the best Christian ever." I grew up thinking that in order for God to love me I had to be worthy of his love. I thought that in order for God to accept me I had to earn my way into his acceptance. I thought that if the leaders in the church or my parents or my grandparents were happy with me, then God must be happy with me too. I didn't understand that the way that God would be happy with, or love me, or accept me, was already taken care of by Christ himself. He had lived perfectly for me. My life, my record, my sins, my "good things" that I did to gain approval, were all hidden in the work of Christ. I was mistakenly trusting in what I would do for myself, or even what I would do for God, in order to reassure myself that I was a Christian.

God is very clear that there will be no earning your way into his family. Being a part of God's family—or being a Christian—is a gift from a generous heavenly Father to his people. You see, I thought I had to earn my relationship with God by following his rules, but that's not what God primarily wants from us.

In the Bible, God always precedes rule-giving with an assurance of his love. Even when God gave the Ten Commandments in Exodus 20, he starts off by saying, "I am GOD, your God, who brought you out of the land of Egypt, out of a life of slavery" (v. 1 MSG). By saying he is our God, he is saying that he loves us and we are his. We have a relationship with him *first*. He tells us what he has done for us: he brought us out of a life of slavery. *Then* he gives us the rules. He doesn't say, "If you follow these rules, *then* I will be your God." He gives himself to us first. He always initiates. He always displays his love through redemption. He did it for the Israelites and he does it for us now. He doesn't wait for us to be worthy, he doesn't wait for us to get our acts together. He just comes toward us with love and unspeakable grace.

First John 4:19b says, "First we were loved, now we love. He loved us first" (MSG). And Titus 3:5a echoes this by saying, "he saved us, not because of works done by us in righteousness, but according to his own mercy . . ."

We are loved first. We aren't loved more if we follow the rules best. We aren't loved more if we are always at church. We aren't loved more if we do our devotional time every single day. We aren't loved more if we get it all right. *We are loved because of who God is, not because of who we are.*

Right about now you might be asking, "What about the rules? I thought we had to try and obey them." My answer to that is yes, of course you should try and obey the rules God gives us. But you don't do it to earn God's love; you do it because you are grateful that you are loved. And if you fail at following the rules, God loves you still.

See, Jesus earned God's unending love *for you* because he was the One who followed every single rule, every day of his life. And now your life, your failures, your successes, are all hidden by Christ's life; when God looks at you, he sees the perfection of Jesus. He sees the One who kept all the rules not because he wanted people to earn people's approval, but because he loved God so very much.

THE JESUS I WANT YOU TO KNOW

The gospel I want you to know is rest. By rest I don't mean take more naps, although I am a big fan of naps; what I mean is that you don't have to work to get God to love you or approve of you. You can stop running. You can catch your breath. Hear me: you don't have to live under the burden that everything depends on you. You cannot follow all the rules, no matter how hard you try. You cannot make everyone happy with you no matter what you do. You cannot earn God's eternal love for you. It is already yours right now.

You can believe God is as good as he says he is. You can stop trying to use the rules to make yourself good. God looks at you right now and says, "You are good because of Jesus."

So, dear friend, rest there. Rest in the work that Christ has done for you. Rest knowing that you are a dearly loved child no matter what you did yesterday, no matter what you do today, and no matter what the future holds. Trust that God is all that he promises to be. Believe that Jesus did all the work for you. Repent of trying to earn your way to God; accept the gift that he has given you. That gift is complete forgiveness, a perfect standing before a holy God, and love everlasting.

DEVOTIONAL QUESTIONS

Read Titus 3:1–11.

1. In the midst of these commands, where do you see evidence of God's love and grace?

2. The author of chapter 13 describes her story of trying to earn God's love. How might you identify with this in your own life?

3. What would it look like for you to rest in God's love?

REST (noun): Freedom from striving. When a person is made righteous by Christ, they no longer have to prove themselves. They can rest in God's grace and Christ's work.

What this means for you: There is nothing you can do to make Jesus love you more than he already does. You can stop running that race. You are fully loved.

Chapter 14
Rejection and the Good News
by David Zahl

I t was a lock, they told me.

The team would meet for its annual post-season banquet. We'd eat some pizza, our coach would hand out a few awards, and then we'd elect next year's captains. I say captains, plural. My sophomore year there had been three. My junior year, two.

Water polo is what you call a niche sport—in New England at least. Sunny places like California and Florida boast robust high school programs, both public and private school leagues. These states tend to feed the US Olympic roster. Up in Connecticut, though, the sport is mainly something for swimmers to do during the off-season. No one takes it that seriously.

When I showed up at boarding school as a new sophomore, I had never played water polo in earnest before. I couldn't tell you the positions, certainly not the rules. I just knew there was a lot of treading water involved. The admissions office must have informed the coach of my facility in the pool, as he wasted no time urging me to go out for the team, assuring me that I'd have a leg up when swim season started that winter. It was a no-brainer, he said.

So out I went, kicking off three seasons of intense play. Turns out that being a good swimmer was more than half the battle. I wasn't going to make any all-American lists, but I more than held my own. By the end of that first year I was starting on varsity, which felt like a big deal. The next fall, I was one of only two juniors who started in every game. The other junior was my good friend Myles.

When captain elections came up, this means there were really only two guys in the running. Fortunately, there had never been less than two captains, so all that remained was to plan my acceptance speech.

You can guess what happened next. The coach tallied the anonymous vote and announced that . . . there would be only one captain next season, and Myles had been chosen.

WHAT?

I was dumbfounded. But it was no prank. Myles looked almost as shocked as I. As the room emptied, everyone avoided eye contact with me, coach included.

Writing about it now, I can still feel a knot form in my belly.

The stakes might seem relatively minor, but at the time, the verdict cut to the core of my seventeen-year-old self.

Most rejections you can write off. You appeal to the "well, I didn't really try that hard" excuse or some form of "who really cares?" In this case, I had tried my hardest for two full seasons. I'd given everything I had and could not pretend I didn't care. There was no way to interpret this rejection other than as a public confirmation of every doubt I'd ever harbored about myself.

You are no leader, my peers had told me. *You do not have what it takes, and we will go out of our way to let you know that.*

It was crushing.

To this day, I have no idea what happened or why. The coach called me that evening but offered no explanation. He just wanted me to know that he could tell I was upset but hoped I would still get in the water next season. Looking back, the nerve of this guy!

The season after I graduated there would be two team captains again, and to my knowledge there have been two captains every year since. Something about me, I could only assume, was so noticeably not-captain-material that tradition had to be suspended.

I remember running into that coach when I was back for a reunion a decade later and fighting the urge to ask about it (or kick him in the shins). These are things you never forget.

THE JESUS I WISH I KNEW IN HIGH SCHOOL

While I had grown up in the church, my relationship with God at the time was complicated. I believed in God, I even believed he loved me. But my father was a pastor, I was far away from home, and the Christians on campus were way too eager. I worried that attending fellowship meetings would hurt my chances with the opposite sex. (It probably would've helped them.)

For whatever reason, I did not turn to God in my shame. Instead, I turned against him. It wasn't because I thought I had let him down somehow, or that he was punishing me. It wasn't even because I had some false notion about God only loving winners.

I knew he was there and I resented him for it.

Meaning, I got mad—at myself for being so un-captain-like and at God for making me that way. Why couldn't I be more like Myles? Maybe in the back of my mind, I knew that God tended not to work through the kind of personal glory a high school senior craved. But my emotional hurt superseded any of that. The rejection ran deep.

It's telling that at no point did I question the authority of my coach and teammates. As far as I was concerned, their authority was ultimate. I had also cut off any fellow Christians who might have pointed out my blind spots. The anger at myself would soon manifest as depression.

You'll note that I haven't mentioned Jesus yet. For whatever reason, I was scared of Jesus in high school. God felt safer. There were less immediate connotations, political or otherwise, when it came to God, more room to maneuver. Jesus, on the other hand, was a lightning rod, and not just among my peers. Committing to him felt infinitely more specific and potentially demanding. To do so risked alienating those who identified with other traditions (or no tradition). And yet, I found that God-without-Jesus didn't have much to say to me in my rejection and anger.

What I would learn a couple of years later—and what I continue to learn to this day—is that a faith without Jesus at its center crumbles. I might not have said as much at the time, but my conception of God-without-Jesus was basically a larger, more powerful version of me; or my father; or worse, an authority figure like my water polo coach.

But the God-revealed-in-Jesus—"the image of the invisible God" as Colossians 1:15 puts it—challenges and even contradicts our expectations of who God should be. We want status. We want favor. We want to impress, and to lead. Yet Jesus was not driven by ego. He was not consumed by what Brené Brown calls "the shame-based fear of being ordinary,"[1] or what I might call "the shame-based fear of not being captain."

Instead, Jesus gave up his position at the right hand of God to mix it up with sinners like you and me. He refused to relate to others on the basis of their performance or popularity; in fact, he seemed most interested in those who had been voted down by society or cast aside (and not always unfairly).

I wish I had known then that God is *not* just like us but bigger, whether that be the worst parts of us or the best. I wish I had grasped the good news of the gospel. Because it is only a God *un*like us—a God unbound by fear or the need for approval—who can save us from ourselves.

This Jesus was rejected by his closest disciples—his teammates, if you will—but he did not reject them in return. His right-hand man Peter flat-out denied knowing Jesus three times, at moments when it might have done either of them some good, and yet Jesus refused to disown Peter after his resurrection.

---

1. Brené Brown, *Daring Greatly: How the Courage to Be Vulnerable Transforms the Way We Live, Love, Parent and Lead* (New York: Gotham, 2012), 22.

Believe it or not, he gave the man more authority rather than less. The least captain-like was appointed captain.

On the cross, Jesus took on the full weight of our faulty judgments, casual cruelties, and thirst for glory, and allowed it to crush him. The One who could walk on water was drowned for the sake of those who had turned against him. This includes you.

THE JESUS I WANT YOU TO KNOW

God is not who you want him to be—and that's okay. More than okay! He does not play by your rules. The voices that echo through the halls of every high school, and sometimes in our own heads, are different from the voice of God. His approval of you is not subject to any vote or public opinion. It is only dependent on the death and resurrection of Jesus.

This means that the rejection you fear—indeed, the rejection you might experience from your peers or from the authority figures in your life—is not the rejection of God.

He would rather reject himself than be alienated from you. As Paul writes in 2 Corinthians 1:18–20a: "As surely as God is faithful, our word to you has not been Yes and No. For the Son of God, Jesus Christ, whom we proclaimed among you, Silvanus and Timothy and I, was not Yes and No; but in him it is always Yes. For all the promises of God find their Yes in him."

For every banquet that goes disastrously wrong in this life, there is one to come in the next life that will not disappoint, where every tearful rejection will be made right and every angry outburst soothed.

Funny as it sounds (and painful as it feels!), every rejection you experience now brings you closer to the heart of God in a way that you can hardly imagine.

Myles and I spoke on the phone recently, twenty years on, and we both agreed that I would've made an insufferable captain. Fortunately, God saved me from what I wanted, and he will save you too.

DEVOTIONAL QUESTIONS

Read Colossians 1:15–20.

1. What do you learn about Jesus through this passage? How has he made all things right?
2. The author of chapter 14 shares his personal experience with rejection. How can you relate?
3. How does Jesus's rejection shape your perspective on approval and status?

ENOUGHNESS (noun): The reality that you lack nothing.

What this means for you: There will be times when you feel inadequate—like you don't quite measure up. The truth is—on your own, you could never measure up. But in Christ, you are more than enough. You lack nothing and are fully accepted by God the Father.

Chapter 15
Conformity and Freedom
by Melina Smith

I n 1992, I was thirteen years old, in the seventh grade, and living the dream. Troll dolls were all the rage; The Cure's "Friday I'm in Love" was number one on the air waves; Will Smith was on the cover of *Teen Magazine*; and I loved Jesus and knew he loved me.

You see, I grew up in Arizona, which is a pretty great place to grow up when you're figuring yourself out. The West provides the illusive freedom of self-discovery. There is no dress code, so I was welcome to try on as many hats (*Blossom* hats included) as I wanted. It felt like real freedom to me—like real Christian freedom.

In the nineties I attended an urban middle school with some rough edges. I had classmates who were in various neighborhood gangs. Some were pregnant, and others went to drinking parties in the desert. I, on the other hand, was a straight-edge, imaginative kid. I followed the rules, lived in my daydreams, and loved my little Arizona life.

I distinctly remember being in first period and trying to figure out why my English partner, Stephanie, was puking most mornings, and why her belly seemed to be growing with each passing month. Like I said, the edges were rough, but I never felt pressured to fit in; I was in the West, after all—the great space where I could be me, walk my own path, totally confident in who Jesus made me to be.

My middle school years flew by and soon I transitioned to Mesa High in 1994, which was in the largest suburban city in Arizona. The new school had all the trappings of a "better" school in a "better" neighborhood. It was made up primarily of kids from well-to-do LDS families (Mormons), and was dominated by a sense of hyper-moralism. Before then, I had never known even a whiff of cultural constraints or moralism or the social elite. Soon, I realized there were new rules to follow, which included the basics I had learned in church. The rules went like this:

1. NO SEX
2. NO DRUGS
3. NO THRASH METAL

And then to really fit in and earn extra social points, you had to follow unspoken and ever-changing rules of what it meant to be "good."

At first I thought to myself, *This should be easy, I got this. I can follow the Golden Rule. I am a Christian. I am a good kid. I will ease right in. Homecoming Queen, here I come!*

After about a semester, I found myself shifting and changing myself to fit in, which I never saw happening. I began to feel like one of those new housing developments—where people and things need to look the same to fit in.

The changes that took shape were subtle at first. I became so agreeable, never wanting to be too different, or to push the norm. I began to notice how different I was from the other kids. My Mexican self suddenly began to hide. Unlike my experience in middle school, I was no longer okay with being different. I became less and less *myself* as I tried to keep up with everyone else. I became less honest about who I was, and pretended to take interest in things I had never even heard of. Slowly over time, the rules began to chip away, and my life began to take the shape of a Caboodle box.

1990's Glossary: A Caboodle box is an oversized beauty product organizer that every teenage girl had. Caboodles have compartments for your scrunchies, your makeup, your jewelry, your crafts, or any other small items you might need to store.

I slowly began to Caboodle my life: I put my faith in Jesus in one compartment, my mixed heritage of being Mexican and Filipino in another compartment, my struggles in another one, and any successes in a different one. Everything was there, but it was tucked away in compartments without any integration. I found myself downplaying the distinctives of my Christian faith with my Mormon friends, which I had never done in middle school. I traded my freedom—a.k.a. the gospel—for a false gospel that had all the trappings of religious *doing*, rather than living or breathing.

It was as if I was trapped in *The Twilight Zone* episode eight, "It's a Good Life."[1] The episode revolves around a small town and family trying to be "good" for a little boy named Anthony. The rules changed constantly, leaving the entire community trapped in fear of being zapped away for not being good enough. Looking back, that is the kind of fear I lived under, the fear of being zapped away. I believed the only way out was to hide and compartmentalize.

My senior year of high school, I gave a speech at graduation. I cringe thinking of it now. A few years ago I listened to it, and could only find sparks of who I am today. I shared jokes that I thought certain friends would appreciate. The entire speech was written to an unknown audience, because I had become unknown to myself. I wish I would have been more secure in the love Christ had over me—the real me.

---

1. *The Twilight Zone*, Season 3, Episode 8, "It's a Good Life," directed by James Sheldon and Rod Serling, November 3, 1961, CBS.

I wish I would have remembered in high school that God is so creative, and he has made us each so uniquely. I had forgotten that God put the stars in the sky, created the jungles, and made me to thrive in Christian freedom. God did not make me to be trapped in a self-made Caboodle.

THE JESUS I WISH I KNEW IN HIGH SCHOOL

The trouble with humans, both teenagers and grown-ups, is that we live with so much fear and anxiety. We are afraid that we will be found unworthy of God's love and zapped away. So we compartmentalize our lives and hide the parts of ourselves that seem inferior. The fear of rejection is powerful, often leaving us paralyzed. It prevents us from acknowledging who we actually are and enjoying the forgiveness we have in Christ.

Looking back at my teen life, I am reminded of Nicodemus. He was part of the religious crew—the Pharisees—battling the "candy crush" of ever-changing rules. Nicodemus and I definitely would have vibed. He neither belonged to the physical rough edges of the world, nor did he really find his place with the elite do-gooders. You get the sense he knew Jesus was the real deal, and that life with him meant freedom. But fear forced him to meet Jesus in the dark of night, like forbidden fruit.

Jesus tells him, "But whoever lives by the truth comes into the light, so that it may be seen plainly that what they have done has been done in the sight of God" (John 3:21 NIV).

I can so relate to Nicodemus. I sensed that Jesus had the goods, the kind of freedom that would allow me the freedom to be myself, to walk into the light. And Nicodemus sensed this too. That is why in the end, even though it was in the dark, Nicodemus snuck off to remove Jesus's body from the cross and take it to a tomb. I had a sense of the real Jesus—I could see it and feel it—but all too often I tucked him and myself away, only to be seen privately in the dark when no one was looking.

I wish I had known that God works with the insecure edges of our lives; the edges—both internal and external—are exactly where Jesus calls us to our true identity. In high school, where everyone was competing for the moral high ground, Jesus simply functioned as a means to an end. He was simply a footnote in our lives. I wish I had known that God wasn't like a teenage boyfriend—in love with you one day and out the next. Or like the capricious, impulsive Anthony from *The Twilight Zone*, ready to zap me away at any moment. God does not vacillate in his feelings toward us; as cheesy as it may sound, God truly is a solid rock, a firm foundation that cannot be shaken

During my middle school life there was no pretension about who was good and who was bad. It was assumed that everyone was working life out, whatever was thrown at them, teen moms and all. That kind of life gave us perspective and the freedom to be ourselves. When you truly see yourself, without fear of being zapped, you can live honestly and transparently, knowing your help comes from God.

THE JESUS I WANT YOU TO KNOW

The gospel I want you to know is that Jesus shows up over and over again for people with rough edges and insecurity. He shows up everywhere, especially in the unexpected places. Jesus rolls in for the blind, the lepers, and the prostitutes. And he's here for "the goodies," and "the baddies," and people like me living that Caboodle life. God made us as individuals and he gives us both the ups and downs so that we might find our help in him.

When you find yourself tucking parts of yourself away—any part—know that Jesus sees it, covers it, and is with you in those places. You see, the God who created and placed the sun, the moon, and the stars in the sky, is the same God who knows you, loves you, and is for you. He is the One who designed the wings of butterflies, who gives us life in full color, who has created you and will meet you wherever you find yourself.

Hang on to the truth that God is hanging on to you, and that while you might have placed all the pieces of your life into the tiny compartments of a Caboodle box, Jesus will put you back together again. He will make you whole so you can walk into the light.

P.S. The piecing together again won't just happen once. Rather, it happens over and over and over again. This is what life is actually all about; it's the tension of what it means to be human.

DEVOTIONAL QUESTIONS
Read John 3:1–21.

1. When Nicodemus comes to meet with Jesus in the dark of night, how does Jesus respond?
2. The author of chapter 15 describes hiding her true self for the sake of being accepted. Have you ever worn a "mask" to fit in?
3. How does the love, grace, and unconditional acceptance of Jesus allow you to walk into the light as one uniquely created by God?

> **WORTHY (noun):** The reality that your life has value.
>
> **What this means for you:** God knew you before the creation of the world. He counted every hair on your head. He knew your name and had a plan for your life. These truths assure you that you are worthy—that your life has meaning. These truths shape who you are.

Chapter 16
Flaws and Faithfulness
by Lauren Hansen

In the spring of 1995 I was thirteen, and I was to meet a boy in the woods.

I have no idea how this meeting was set up. I only recall that I thought he liked me. And that opportunity for affirmation was enough for me. I told my babysitter I was going to go on a walk. I blow-dried my hair and then swept it up behind a perfectly placed headband. I put on a full face of makeup and made sure to select the most kissable lip gloss. I picked out my wardrobe to look pretty and feminine: a white blouse with sky-blue embroidered flowers at the top and my best jeans to match. Finally, I examined myself in the mirror, took a deep breath, and headed out the door.

We were to meet in the woods at a boulder the size of a Chevy; I arrived at the location first. I positioned myself so that the light coming through the trees would perfectly frame my face, while I casually leaned up against the rock. After a few minutes, I heard him approach.

It was all over quickly.

He greeted me, asked how I was, and then he left.

Nothing happened.

What was that? I thought. *He must not like me. Why doesn't he like me?* Then I firmly concluded, *It must have been how big my hips looked leaning up against that rock.*

Self-worth is a tricky find. Ever since I can remember, I wanted to be loved. I craved to be loved. I searched high and low in all the wrong places. I thought that love had to be earned, that I had to be what people wanted in order to get their love in return. And if I could just mold myself into their expectations, then I'd find what I so desired.

I thought if I got good grades, my teachers and administrators would love me. So I made straight As. I thought if I excelled in an extracurricular activity, I'd earn praise from parents and peers. So I was on the dance team. I thought if I looked like a magazine cover model, I'd be the envy of every girl and the desire of every boy. So I starved myself.

Anorexia was the sharp tool I used to carve the best image of me. I quickly learned that I could shape myself into smaller-sized clothes, starve myself into jealous compliments, and harm myself into the sixteen-year-old ideal. I have never received more compliments in my life than when I was dangerously underweight. All that affirmation cloaked the ugly truth of my addiction. I would lie, flake out, judge others, suffer mood swings, and feel consistent physical pain, all for the sake of love and acceptance. My mom, a former model herself, took me to a modeling agency to assess me as potential talent. What would they change about me before putting me onto the runway? They'd pluck my eyebrows.

I had come that close to "perfection."

And it was totally empty.

My desires and efforts were crushing. *If I eat this forbidden food, will my body grow larger, and will I lose love? If they really knew me, would they like me at all? Do I even like myself?* My mind constantly raced with calculations of doing enough. Getting 100 percent on a quiz, not missing one move on the dance team and, of course, not eating anything beyond my list of acceptable food and caloric intake, which must have been only enough to feed a fish. I ran myself ragged to be perfect and to be enough.

And I actually got darn close to meeting the world's standards.

Until it all came crashing down.

Thanksgiving night of my senior year in high school my family members were out of the house, so I was alone, just me versus the sweet potato casserole—my favorite Thanksgiving dish. The brown sugar, pecans, and butter, with a few yams hidden underneath. Of course, with my eating disorder, I had not had sweet potato casserole in many-a-Thanksgiving. But my unflinching self-control failed me in that moment, all alone in the house on a chilly fall evening. I ate a bite of sweet potatoes. Then a few more bites after that. And then I immediately began calculating how to negate my lapse in judgment. I decided I'd go on a run. But with the weather, I could not go outside, so I decided I would jog a loop *inside* my house. Great plan!

I turned on TVs in multiple rooms, and cruised around the house while watching *Ferris Bueller's Day Off*. So I'm jogging and congratulating myself on what a whiz I am at this whole perfection thing, and then I see my cat. My sweet kitty had saucer-sized black eyes. He was terrified. *Of me*. Something about that moment, jogging around my house while my cat looked on in horror made me realize for the first time that I had lost control of myself.

What do we do when we realize that we've put our hope in all the wrong places? It's a very humbling situation, isn't it? You think you're all you've got. You think you can handle it. You think your whole life rests on your shoulders. And then you fail. It was in this precise moment of failure when God came to save me.

THE JESUS I WISH I KNEW IN HIGH SCHOOL

A friend invited me to a Bible study on the book of John for a small group of high school seniors. I had never read the Bible, except for treating it like a Magic 8-Ball from time to time and receiving answers that never made much sense. The parables that I would flip to without fail always tripped me up. But for the first time in that Bible study, I read the whole story of Jesus, and John 3:16 finally made the gospel come alive to me: "For God so loved the world, that he gave his only Son, that whoever believes in him should not perish but have eternal life." It struck me: for God so loved *me* that he'd given up his Son, his only Son, to win *me*. *Me*! It may sound overly simplistic, but that truth was the affirmation I'd always searched for; from the moment that verse clicked, I was saved and on the path to physical healing, just weeks into the Bible study.

What I needed—a Savior—I had; and it had nothing to do with my appearance or efforts. My worth, bigger and more beautiful than I ever imagined it could be, was a gift from God. I had nothing to do but accept it. Everything else paled in comparison to the light and gift of Christ.

The Jesus who revealed himself to me with only a few short weeks of high school remaining is the Jesus I wish I'd known in all of high school. He gave me a renewed mind. I thought that I could not be acceptable without *earning* acceptance. I thought I'd always have to strive in order to be liked. I thought that if I ever truly let people in, they'd find something they didn't like and would abandon me. I thought that life was a masquerade ball where we were all just shuffling around, attracted to the shiniest mirage.

Jesus is different. I am acceptable because he calls me accepted. I don't have to strive to be liked; I am so loved that God gave me his Son. I can let people in, because the only Person I truly needed let me in and he will never abandon me. I'm a sojourner in this fallen world with the Lord walking beside me all the way to heaven.

Christian, we are totally loved by God through Christ, and it has nothing to do with being pleasing through physical appearance. God designed us, created us, and sent his only begotten Son to die for us. Why? Because he loves us. God's love is different: it can't be earned and won't stop for anything. We could be Instagram perfection, or we could hardly get a single "like"—neither of those realities change God's abiding love, adoration, and approval of us one bit.

THE JESUS I WANT YOU TO KNOW

Friend, lay down your striving. You do not have to earn your worth. As a child of God, you are worthy beyond calculation. Find your rest in your identity in Christ, and strive no more under the heavy weight of looking right, fitting in, or being perfectly pleasing. As a Christian, God looks at you and sees Christ. You are without stain or blemish. You are adored. Know that Jesus counts you worthy. And, when in doubt, look to the love he showed you on the cross.

DISCUSSION QUESTIONS

Read John 3:16.

1. How would you define the word *world*? Are you included in God's proclamation of love for the whole world?
2. What parts of yourself—physically or otherwise—do you wish were different?
3. If God created you perfectly in his image, how does this transform the way that you see yourself, particularly the things you can't change? What if you tried to see yourself the way God sees you—created with love and attention, and beautifully clothed in Jesus's perfect righteousness?

NEW HEAVENS/NEW EARTH (nouns): At the end of time, Christ will return to the earth, and all will be made perfect. The heavens and earth will join together as one, like Eden.

What this means for you: This world is not your true home; it is not the end of your story. You have an eternal story awaiting you in paradise, where everything wrong will be made right—where there will be no more tears, sickness, or sadness. No matter what you face each day, you have this certain hope of what's to come. This is only the beginning.

Chapter 17
Fear and Courage
by Scott Sauls

I still remember the feeling I had walking into my first day of high school.

I was afraid.

Would people like me? Or would they ignore me, or worse, make fun of me? Would they notice the acne on my face, or my big goofy hair, or how embarrassingly skinny I was? Well, of course they would. But would I be punished, bullied, or mistreated for these things—things I had no power to change?

It didn't take long to get an answer to the question my fears were asking. The answer was *yes*.

In my freshman fitness class, it didn't take long for my tall, lanky body to earn me the nicknames "Stick" and "Q-Tip." The coach who taught the class gave me both of these names. During the same semester, the prettiest girl in homeroom—the girl I had a secret crush on at the time—nominated me to represent our homeroom in the annual "Mister Pretty Legs" contest.

Wanting to be a good sport, I accepted the prettiest girl's nomination. Two weeks later, all of us who were nominated wore shorts to school. The contest was held during a pep rally at lunch time. When it was their turn, each contestant would step on stage in front of the entire school and be scored by how loudly their fellow students, including freshmen, sophomores, juniors, and seniors, cheered. Ken, who ran track and played varsity football and had Olympic thighs, quads, and calves, went right before me. Predictably, the student body cheered with loud, passionate approval as Ken flexed his perfectly chiseled, muscular legs.

Then, it was my turn. My fellow students' roaring cheers turned into roaring laughter. There I stood, the joke of the school—the six foot five, 130-pound stick—mortified. The pretty girl nominated me not out of admiration for my legs, but to ensure that everyone could get a good laugh at my expense. It was humiliating.

From that point forward, I told myself that I would do anything for that sort of thing to never happen to me again. Whatever it took, I would deflect attention away from my weakest and most embarrassing feature (or so I had been taught to think)—my body type—by becoming special, unique, a stand-out of some sort.

My first attempt at standing out was to try the class clown route. I disrespected my teachers in class, making jokes instead of taking the class seriously. It got me some detentions and some warnings, but it felt worth it because of the positive attention I was getting from my classmates. Instead of teasing me for my skinny frame, they were laughing at my disrespectful jokes. One day, my humor stooped to its lowest low when I looked across the room at a girl named Ann, and in front of everyone said, "Hey Ann! You are the ugliest girl I have ever seen!" Ann was devastated, but the whole class laughed. And since the whole class laughed, I did it again, except this time to Dean. "Hey Dean!" I said, "You are the dumbest boy I've ever known!" Again, the class laughed, but Dean was humiliated.

Truthfully, I walked away from class that day feeling dirty and ashamed. Even now, as a middle-aged adult, I feel horrible about what I did to Ann and Dean that day. I had been so desperate for attention, so desperate for approval, and so desperate not to be made fun of or bullied myself, that I had *become* a bully.

Next time you see a mean girl being mean, or a bully being a bully, remind yourself that mean girls are mean and bullies are bullies not because they feel good about themselves, but because they feel bad about themselves. Like me in high school, they are scared. Scared of rejection, scared of being invisible, scared of feeling like they don't matter. Sometimes we are tempted to do some pretty awful things when we feel scared.

Even after I quit trying to be a class clown, I still had my fears. I looked for other things besides being funny to tell me I was special, something to deflect attention away from my insecurity, my skinny body, my bushy hair, and all the other things that made me feel ashamed and afraid. So I turned to athletics, having a girlfriend, making better grades, and whatever else would help numb my ever-present social fears. But without Jesus, if I'm being honest, I was never able to shake my fear of rejection.

Many years later I watched the movie *Wonder*[1] with our two teenage daughters. (If you haven't seen the movie, I highly recommend it!) The movie did a spectacular job telling the truth about how hard it is being a teenager. The hero of the story is Auggie and, like me in high school, he had lots of fears and insecurities and had been made fun of about his physical appearance. At the end of the film, he summarizes the experience of every single student, whether popular or invisible, beautiful or average looking, jocks or cheerleaders, academics or chess club members; he says to be kind to everyone, because everyone is fighting a hard battle.

THE JESUS I WISH I KNEW IN HIGH SCHOOL

When I was in high school, I did not know Jesus like I know him now. I wish I had, because I would have known that I was not alone. I would have known that the One who *made* my skinny

---

1. *Wonder*, directed by Stephen Chbosky (2017; Santa Monica, CA: Lionsgate, 2018), DVD.

body made me with purpose, and that he did not see me as a Stick or a Q-Tip or a reason to burst out into roaring laughter. Instead, he saw me as fearfully and wonderfully made (Psalm 139:14), the apple of his eye (Psalm 17:8), and the crown of his creation (Psalm 8:1–8), created in the image of God (Genesis 1:27).

If I had known Jesus Christ in high school, I would have also known that I didn't have to perform or make myself special by being funny or winning championships or becoming the MVP of a team. I would have known that he *already* delighted in me, not because of anything smart or funny or amazing that I had done, but simply because of his character.

He takes great delight in me (Zephaniah 3:17), is not ashamed of me (Hebrews 2:11), watches over me (Psalm 121:5–8), is always with me (Matthew 28:20), will never leave me (Hebrews 13:5), has adopted me (Romans 8:15–16), and is a friend who sticks closer than a brother (Proverbs 18:24).

And? He has forgiven me for even the worst, meanest, dumbest, most hurtful things I have ever done. When he could condemn me, shame me, laugh at me, and dismiss me like the whole student body did that day—when he could say, "Hey Scott! You're ugly!" or "Hey Scott! You're dumb!"—he does no such thing. Instead, he says to me, "Hey Scott! I love you! You matter! I'm proud of you! I want to be with you! I want you to know how special you are to me, and that there is nothing you can do to change that! I want you to know that I love you at all times, at your best and at your worst!"

With a friend like Jesus in high school, I imagine that I would not have felt such a need to protect myself from the things and people I feared most. In fact, I might have actually become an encourager to my fellow students who felt the same fears that I did. Because when Jesus draws close to us, he encourages us—*he puts courage into us*—so we can set our fears under the umbrella of his love and care, and encourage others.

Had I known Jesus in high school, I imagine also that I would have realized, at least on some level, that being funny and good-looking and popular and cool are fine and good as long as we don't hurt others; at the same time they are pretty overrated. In the end, it's kindness, like Auggie in *Wonder* lived—as opposed to being funny and good-looking and popular and cool—that will make the biggest difference. In fact, the older I get, the more convinced I become that being kind is so much better than being popular or cool. Because while being popular and cool might keep you from getting laughed at in high school, being kind is what will help you win at life. And the earlier you start, the more remarkable and filled with *wonder* your life will be.

Cool might win high school. But kindness wins life. So, be kind then, because everyone you meet is fighting a hard battle.

I imagine that if I had been close to Jesus in high school, I would not have cared about being funny, and I would have tried to encourage my classmates—to put courage into them—instead of taking courage from them, by laughing at their expense.

I'm pretty sure that would have been the case. I wish, therefore, that I had started with Jesus much, much earlier in my life. As the book of Ecclesiastes says, it is always best to get serious about God and get close to Jesus "in the days of your youth" (12:1).

THE JESUS I WANT YOU TO KNOW

What I wish I had known—and what I want for you—is to know that you matter to God, and there is nothing you can do to change that. He cannot love you more than he already does, and he will not love you less. Because of Jesus, God approves of you and will love you for all eternity.

Maybe this is why the most repeated command in the Bible is, "Do not fear." Specifically, the Bible says this 365 times—once for each day of the year. The reason you and I don't have to fear any more is that in Jesus, God is for us, and God is with us.

I hope this, more than anything else, will give you courage. And I hope that in gaining the courage that comes from Jesus, you will also become kind.

DEVOTIONAL QUESTIONS

Read Zephaniah 3:14–17.

1. How are you comforted by these words?
2. The author of chapter 17 bullied people out of fear and insecurity. Where do you find yourself acting out of fear and insecurity?
3. How does knowing the grace and affection of God help you to encourage others?

PERFORMANCE (noun): Accomplishing or fulfilling an act, task, or function.

What this means for you: It's tempting to make a name for yourself—in grades, friendships, and performance. It's tempting to prove your worth. Even as a Christian, you can be tempted by religious performance. But your performance can never make God love you more. And there's nothing you can do that would make him love you less. You are secure in his love, regardless of how well you perform.

Chapter 18
Shame and Holiness
by Kevin Yi

At the church I grew up in, our congregation would pick one weekend in the spring to have our Sunday service at an outdoor park. This was an opportunity for our community groups to picnic together, and to play games for prizes and rewards. The youth group would always have our own time for outdoor activities and games, and we would end early enough to watch our parents participate in their games. The adult games were usually pretty tame, and we'd stand around and make fun of the older adults as they attempted tug-of-rope, three-legged-races, or digging for candy in piles of flour.

One particular year, I did something that I consider to be a trophy on the mantel of my lifetime's epic fails. As usual, our youth group played our own games at the beginning of the picnic, and when we made our way up the hill back to the main field where the adults were playing theirs, we saw 800 adults on their hands and knees crawling on the grass, looking for something that had obviously been lost.

What kind of lame game is this? I thought. *You know what would be funny? Whatever it is they're looking for, I should pretend that I found it!*

And just like that, I ran into the sea of adults on their hands and knees, and shouted at the top of my lungs in Korean, "찾았어요 (*Cha jah ssuh yo*—I found it)!" And when all of the adults looked up at me, I just laughed and said, "No, I was just kidding!"

No. One. Laughed.

My youth pastor grabbed my arm and very quickly explained that one of our congregants had lost their incredibly expensive diamond ring, and all of the willing adults had spent the last twenty minutes combing the field area for it during lunch prep.

The blood drained from my face.

I had made this incredibly stupid faux pas in front of, literally, the entire church. I eventually made the walk of shame to my parents' community group picnic area, and it was a frosty reception. I felt like a deep disappointment to my parents that day. I had embarrassed them in front of our whole community. My desire to be funny had brought shame on my family and, once again, I failed to live up to unspoken expectations of what brings honor to my parents.

Honor and shame. Growing up in a Korean home, these were the two guiding principles for understanding my relationship with my parents and their community of influence, especially at church. This means that it was my duty as a faithful son to do whatever I could to make sure that my parents appeared to be excellent, honorable parents who raised obedient, successful children. Whatever ideas I had about my own happiness and joy were frowned upon if that meant compromising my parents' standing in the community. So getting good grades, being accepted to Harvard, and receiving scholarships? Heaps of honor. Mess up at a piano recital or get in trouble at school for reckless and embarrassing behavior? Piles of shame.

Now, I don't blame my parents for this dynamic. By itself, this dynamic is not bad. Bringing honor to my parents is a biblical command, and to avoid doing things that would bring them shame is also a wise way to live. But within this framework, I came to view my relationship with God in the same exact way.

I assumed God was happy with me when I brought him honor and did explicitly Christian things—like evangelize, attend church events, earn good grades, and exemplify good character. But what happened when I looked at pornography, cheated on an assignment, or failed to do my quiet time? Certainly, I brought shame upon myself and upon God.

At times when I felt particularly shameful, I thought it best to take a break from my relationship with God. I thought I first needed to work on improving myself, and then I could come to him with my accomplishments and hopefully make up for my mistakes.

As a teenager, this was my understanding of how things worked. Jesus was the doorway to a relationship with God, but once I was saved, it was on me to prove my worth to him every single day. And I carried this mindset all throughout my high school and college years. It led me through tiresome and draining cycles of love and hate with the Lord. On one hand, I knew he loved me and I wanted to love him; on the other hand, I never felt as though I was good enough to truly be accepted.

My relationship with God was always based on how I viewed my own performance. When I thought I was honoring God through my actions, I was secure. But when I was living in ways that were shameful, I was filled with doubt.

THE JESUS I WISH I KNEW IN HIGH SCHOOL

It took me a very long time to recognize that this way of thinking was not consistent with the gospel. God used an Old Testament story, the account of Israel's most famous sin, to open my eyes to his magnificent, shame-busting gospel. It's the story of the Golden Calf, found in Exodus 32. God's people are just starting out on their journey across the wilderness to the Promised Land; they have just been freed from slavery in Egypt.

In this particular scene, the Israelites are parked in front of Mount Sinai, and they've just committed themselves to following God's law. God then invites Moses to join him on the mountain, to receive the tablets of the law. But when Moses has been gone for quite some time, God's people rebel against Aaron, who is Moses's older brother and second in command. They demand that Aaron make them new gods to lead them. (It turns out, you can take the people out of Egypt, but you can't take Egypt out of the people.)

How do you think Aaron responds? Does he tell them to have patience? Nope. Does he tell them that making new gods is a bad idea? Nope.

He promptly gives in, gathers up all of their gold jewelry, melts it down, fashions a calf, and declares it to be their new god.

Moses is immediately alerted to the Israelites' sin, and he rushes back down the mountain to witness the ensuing chaos as Israel descends into idolatry. When Moses confronts his brother about what happened, Aaron fumbles around and says that he took the Israelites' gold and "threw it into the fire, and out came this calf" (Exodus 32:24). The story continues, ". . . Moses saw that the people had broken loose (for Aaron had let them break loose, to the derision of their enemies)" (v. 25). It hit me: Aaron's actions had caused all of Israel to fall into sin, and therefore bring shame to the people of God and God himself. Instead of the word *derision*, the CSB and NIV translations of the Bible say that Israel had become a "laughingstock," and in the Message paraphrase, a *disgrace*.

Deep in my soul, I get Aaron. Because I am Aaron.

Like Aaron, I have been an embarrassment to myself, my church, my friends, and my family. I've messed up so many times—and failed in such spectacularly un-Christlike ways— that I have felt deeply unworthy to be called a Christian.

Aaron's story doesn't end here.

Moses prays on behalf of Aaron, and God not only spares his life, but the next time we see Aaron in Exodus 39, he is being clothed in holy, priestly garments—designed exclusively for the priests. These garments were made with the finest materials, and were decorated with precious stones that represented the twelve tribes of Israel. But it is the description of Aaron's crown that really catches my attention. Exodus 28:36 says, "You shall make a plate of pure gold and engrave on it, like the engraving of a signet, 'Holy to the LORD.'"

This means that the highlight of the priestly garment was a crown that showed off to all of Israel: the wearer of this crown is unique, special, precious, to be set apart for the Lord. You see, Jesus is the greater Moses, who prays on our behalf so that we would be presented before God as "Holy to the LORD." Just as Aaron is clothed in the finest robes and presented before all of the Israelites, so we are robed in Christ's righteousness, the crowning glory before the entire universe (see Ephesians 2:4–9).

This changed everything. I finally understood that God's grace for me is not something he had to do as some kind of obligation. The Father's grace for me is truly lavish and shocking. Had I really understood this as a teenager, I would have spent less time trying to earn my standing before God, and more time enjoying the relationship that was available to me through Jesus Christ. Rather than seeing my spiritual practices of prayer, Bible reading, and volunteering at church as ways to receive God's acceptance, I could have experienced all of those things as a way to enjoy his presence. And during the times when things were hard for me, I wouldn't have viewed it as some kind of harsh punishment for my sinful behavior, but rather, I could have gone through those difficult times knowing that Jesus was with me through my suffering.

THE JESUS I WANT YOU TO KNOW

Reader, because of what Jesus has done on your behalf, you never have to question God's unending love and care for you. He is forever invested in your salvation. He does not shame you, but has eternally dignified you and promised a great inheritance through Jesus. Just like Aaron, because of Jesus, you and I are no longer the chief of sinners—we are holy and set apart, prepared to do the work of the kingdom of God with gratitude and passion.

DEVOTIONAL QUESTIONS

Read Exodus 28:36–38.

1. How might you describe the God who, instead of punishing Aaron, clothes him with holy robes and a plate of gold?

2. The author of chapter 18 describes his desire to behave well for both God and his family. Have you ever felt similarly, or distant from God when you failed?

3. Because of the grace of Jesus, what does God *actually* think of you when you fail?

THE HONOR/SHAME WORLDVIEW (noun): Honor—Shame is a way that many cultures see the world. Honor is given to people who act in line with a shared social code; anyone who fails to live up to that code has shame placed upon them. We see this most often in social media interactions, where we have to be careful what we post, lest we get "cancelled." This worldview can sometimes curb bad behavior, but it can also leave us feeling deeply unworthy.

What this means for you: The gospel is good news for this worldview because your identity and worth are no longer dependent on you doing all of the right things. You are now secure in what Christ has done for you. Though you will stumble and fail often, you will never be "cancelled" by God because the gospel says that you are a beloved child of God.

Chapter 19
Disability and Suffering
by Rachel Kang

I felt broken, like everything around me was broken. My body was broken. My family was broken. My future was broken. Every dream I ever had for my life—broken.

There I was, sitting in a silent room with the echoing sound of a diagnosis still fresh on my doctor's lips. "Rheumatic fever," he'd said. "It's an autoimmune disease caused by untreated strep throat. It's when your body attacks your own body. It causes arthritis in the joints. And, sometimes, it can cause failure of the heart," he explained.

I heard the doctor's voice and knew that he was talking to me. But all I could think in that moment was how my body felt heavy and light, cold and hot, frozen and flushed—all at the same time. *I was nervous.* And, suddenly, the thoughts came rushing in. *What did this mean for my life? What was happening? Would I be okay?*

I was only in ninth grade—I was young and life wasn't supposed to go this way. I wasn't supposed to have swelling in my joints or the possibility of sickness in my heart. I should have been dreaming about the possibilities of my future, not dreading the reality that my body was broken and in need of healing.

He told me the treatments would be mailed to my house in Styrofoam containers. He told me I'd have to schedule appointments to see him every time a container came to my house.

And so I did just that—I made my appointments and carried my Styrofoam containers with me to each visit. I'd walk to the silent room and lay on the table with the crinkling paper until I felt the cold needle shoot deep into my bottom. I would stare at the wall, stare into the silence of that room, and hope for the medicine to work like magic. Hope for my heart to be saved and for my dreams to be spared.

With a weakened voice, broken and beat down from my bout with strep throat and rheumatic fever, I spent the final months of my freshman year unable to sing in the choir and unable to scream chants with my cheer squad. I spent those months mouthing the words at every chorus practice and sitting out of every game.

So I decided that, in the meantime, I would write my own songs—songs that allowed my voice to sing with the little strength it had. In my room, I'd gaze at the magazine covers of Pink, Avril Lavigne, Britney Spears, and Christina Aguilera plastered across the wall over my keyboard. It was here where I began to write the song I later called "Poison." On the piano, my finger pads moved across keys of white and black, while the words came from deep inside of me:

> I can feel it, I know whenever it's there
> On my lips, on my tongue, I can feel it tear
> At the voice, that sings so strongly
> So weak, so fatigued, I can't go on.

I wrote the song with minor chords, with riffs of emotion. Anger welled up in my body, deeper than my physical pain. I realized—I wasn't so much angry at being disabled, as I was of being deprived of the deepest dream I'd ever had.

To sing.

How could God take away the one dream I ever had? How could God, whom I had come to know and trust with my heart, strike me with sickness and steal away the one thing that meant the most to me? Up until this point, I had easily believed everything I ever learned about God. I had believed that he was good and that he could heal the sick.

But hearing the news of my diagnosis changed everything. I began believing that if brokenness touched my life and body, then brokenness must be the way of God—his design, desire, and dream for my life.

This wasn't my first encounter with brokenness. I experienced it while watching my older brother live with brain damage. It came in the fractures that I saw pull at my parents' marriage, and when death robbed me of my loving aunt and beloved grandmother.

I surged with pain and confusion. I felt lost in a fog and I feared for the future. If God was good, why was life so bad? If God was good, why did he allow more hurt than healing? Why did he cripple my brother? Why did he bring more suffering than he did solace?

THE JESUS I WISH I KNEW IN HIGH SCHOOL

When I return to this—my story—to the brokenness of my past, I can't help but wish I had known a different Jesus in high school. I can't help but think about how maybe it wasn't healing that I needed, but for someone to tell me that I wasn't beyond wholeness or hope.

When I look back, I see sorrow and sadness in the eyes of a girl who was physically and spiritually sick. I was blinded and debilitated, utterly unable to see or believe the truth about God, and particularly the truth about Jesus.

Maybe, if I had lived with eyes and heart wide open, I would have believed Jesus to be more than just some good guy from the Bible. I would have seen him for the broken body that he himself bore as he died the cruelest death on that old rugged cross—*for me.*

This Jesus who I thought I had figured out, who I thought had fit neatly and nicely in the lines of all those coloring pages I scribbled across as a kid, is more than what meets the eye. More than some superficial superhero, Jesus is a man of sorrows—a blameless man who entered into a broken world that, in turn, broke and bruised him. Isaiah 53:2–3a (NIV) says,

> He grew up before him like a tender shoot,
>   and like a root out of dry ground.
> He had no beauty or majesty to attract us to him,
>   nothing in his appearance that we should desire him.
> He was despised and rejected by mankind,
>   a man of suffering, and familiar with pain.

Jesus, a man willing to be beaten and left to bleed, even to the point of death—who died to bring all things together—not only suffered for me, but suffered *like me*? Suffered *with me*?

If I had known this, if I had known that Jesus's purpose wasn't to merely promise healing but to portray his presence, his closeness, I would have seen him shouldering my pain more than my soul-sick eyes had strained to see.

I would have spent less time wandering and more time in wonder. Less time reaching for healing, and more time simply reaching for him. For his hereness, for his presence. If I had seen the person of Jesus, I would have seen God's good purpose for my life and for this world—God's Son who not only sympathizes with our brokenness, but empathizes with it.

It is not wrong to reach for healing. Healing is a gift. But, that's just it—it's a gift and not a guarantee.

Our world is broken and filled with broken things. Bodies will break; families will break; marriages will break; souls, minds, and hearts will break. And healing on this side of heaven—whether it be physically, mentally, or emotionally—is a gift. It is only one of the many ways he chooses to show us that he cares for us.

But grace? That's a guarantee. God's forgiveness bestowed upon us—by and through Christ's death and resurrection—is a guarantee. And, more than giving us things and goods and gifts, God's greatest desire—his greatest dream—is that we might come to the place of receiving him. That, in the midst of living in this weary world, we remember the Christ who came—fully in flesh—to bring spiritual healing to our souls.

To receive the truth of Jesus's broken body—that he suffered with us, like us, and for us—is the greatest gift.

I know this, because I've lived it. Even now, I have flashbacks of the moments I spoke up and out about the grace and gift of God despite the existence of sickness in my body. I let my pain pale in comparison to the power of knowing and believing in God's greatest gift—Jesus. In him, I have all that I need; my heart is secure and my soul is satisfied.

THE JESUS I WANT YOU TO KNOW

Beloved of God, here is what I want you to know deep in your bones, a truth to hold that feels closer than your skin. That Jesus hears every prayer and heals in more ways than one. Look for him in that space within your heart that was once numb but is now filled with love. Look for him in the ways you've learned to wait. Look for him in the sunset, in the way the trees dance and sway.

And know, your body—imperfect and finite—is not your final resting place. Someday, you will rise—wholly raised with holy strength—and enjoy eternity with a body perfected and redeemed, just like God promised (see Romans 8:18–25). On this side of that promise, know that no darkness, no death, and no amount of damage can ever separate you from the dream—the burning desire—that God has for you, which is to be with you.

He wants you just as you are, and can use you just as you are. He wants to fill you just as you are, and can satisfy you just as you are.

He'll spark and inspire new dreams within you—of which the greatest is to draw closer to himself—even after your own dreams have been destroyed.

So, see this grace. And chase it down more than any other thing. He loves you just as you are—broken, beloved, and beautiful. You are worthy and worth it. In Christ, you are bound for eternity and everlasting belonging.

DEVOTIONAL QUESTIONS

Read Romans 8:18–25.

1. Can you picture "the glory that will be revealed in us" in eternity? What broken parts of your own body or life will be healed in heaven? What about the groaning world around you? Take a minute to imagine the new heavens and new earth, where all sad things will come untrue.
2. The author of chapter 19 describes her anger at God over suffering. Have you ever felt angry at God? How does Christ's own suffering shape your perspective?
3. How might the promise of Jesus to make all things new transform your anger into hope?

MAN OF SORROWS (proper noun): Isaiah 53:3a predicts that many years before the birth of Christ, the Messiah would be "despised and rejected by men, a man of sorrows and acquainted with grief."

What this means for you: You can take comfort that this Jesus, the Lover and Creator of your soul, knows intimately what it is to suffer, to be rejected by his peers, and to feel despair. God is not distant or unfamiliar with your problems. He is nearer than you know.

Chapter 20
Faith and God's Seal
by Emily Heide

W hen I was in the eighth grade, five high school sophomores were in a terrible car accident after youth group
one Sunday. Four of them walked out with minor cuts and
bruises, but Courtney did not survive. To say this tragedy shook
up our church would be an understatement. Anytime someone
young dies unexpectedly, the mourning, anguish, and grief is
deep and sudden.

Two weeks later, our youth group went on a retreat called
Breakaway. The weekend was vulnerable, raw, and emotional
for us all. I struggled with how God could allow something so
terrible to happen. At the same time, I wanted to know that if
I met the same fate, I was loved by the Lord and would have a
place in his heavenly kingdom.

On the last night of the retreat at the conclusion of our worship time, the retreat leader asked anyone who was willing to
put their faith in Jesus to approach the altar and pray with him.
Along with many of my friends, I made my way up to the front,
knelt under the hands of adult leaders, and was prayed over.
In that moment, I believed that Christ had taken my sin upon
himself on the cross. I believed that because of his perfect life,
death, and resurrection, I was now fully forgiven; I became part

of God's family. It was a transcendent moment, and tears rolled down my face. At that point in time, I loved the Lord and desperately longed for him to change my heart, heal the pain, and make me new.

After the retreat, I continued on my path of the straight-and-narrow, attending church, hand bells, choir, and youth group, as well as any and all mission trips and retreats. I was hopeful that my new heart would instantly replace my sinful tendencies—primarily self-righteousness and gossip—with the fruits of the Spirit.   .

But it wasn't as quick and easy as I had anticipated. Why was I still tempted to sin if the Holy Spirit resided in my heart? Why wasn't I seeing the changes I was promised? Instead of love, joy, peace, patience, gentleness, kindness, faithfulness, and self-control, temptations became harder to resist. I had been taught that Jesus died for my sins, but I was confused by the quickly accruing sin in my life. I had no framework for talking to God about my sins, or for receiving his grace. So I did the only thing that seemed natural—I hid.

I began to doubt my salvation and faith altogether. I stopped reading the Bible, praying, and attending church. If I was truly a Christian, wouldn't my sinful nature have vanished the day I put my trust in Christ?

In college, one of my wildest and party-girl friends asked me about Jesus. She had known about my faith years earlier and was curious. Over the course of the next six weeks, I watched her accept the love of Jesus and dramatically change everything in her life. She stopped drinking, going to parties, and staying out all hours of the night. She started studying the Bible, attending church, praying, and telling anyone who would listen about her new heart and love for Jesus.

Watching her transformation, I felt frustrated and betrayed. I had trusted in Jesus too; why did he not cause that kind of immediate change in my own heart? Did God even renew my heart in the first place? Why didn't my story look as dramatic and exciting as hers? Did God love me the same way he loved her? Did I ever even really believe?

I finally revealed my struggles to a small group of Christian friends. They explained to me that the gospel was about God's unmerited love for all sinners. In this fallen world, we all sin. That will not change this side of heaven, but over time God will work in our hearts, drawing us closer to him, and making us more like him. They taught me about living for the glory of God alone—not for myself and my own righteousness.

After a long period of struggle, I finally turned to God and prayed, "Help my unbelief" (see Mark 9:23–24). I also began spending more time with him in prayer, Scripture, and worship. And, very slowly, the Lord began to work in my heart. He showed me that *he* was the one I needed to approach with my insecurities and doubts. I learned to differentiate between the desires of my flesh and the desires of God. I learned how to repent of my sin and receive the grace of God. All of this has drawn me into a deeper and closer relationship with the Lord. I have come to more clearly see the truths of his character.

My ongoing sanctification, or being set apart for God, has been a long journey (with many seasons and moments of fear and doubt along the way). But I continue to lean on our Lord, and he continues to bless and work in me through challenges, grief, suffering, and the everyday mundane moments too. He is, in his time, making my heart more like his.

THE JESUS I WISH I KNEW IN HIGH SCHOOL

In high school, I wish I had known that the very moment I gave my life to the Lord, no one and nothing—not my sin, not my doubts—could change the reality that I was his.

The apostle Paul says in his letter to the Ephesians, "When you heard the word of truth, the gospel of your salvation, and believed in him, [you] were sealed with the promised Holy Spirit" (1:13).

In the days of Jesus, a seal was something deemed important by the sender and receiver of a letter. It qualified the communication as authentic, as well as the letter itself intact. For believers, that seal is the Holy Spirit: the undeniable work of God in and for us, bearing witness to our identity as adopted sons and daughters of the Most High King, and coheirs with Christ (Romans 8:17), set apart as holy (1 Peter 2:9).

Whether our conversion happens in a dramatic altar call or in the quiet confines of our own bedrooms, it makes no difference. We are his.

The apostle Paul's conversion story begins on the road to Damascus, where Jesus meets him and blinds him. After three days, the Lord sends Ananias to lay his hands on Paul, restoring his sight. "And immediately he proclaimed Jesus in the synagogues . . . increased all the more in strength, and confounded the Jews who lived in Damascus by proving that Jesus was the Christ" (Acts 9:20a, 22). Paul's conversion is dramatic, and the change in his heart seemingly instantaneous.

This is a story I remember repeatedly hearing in Sunday school and always being awestruck, almost ashamed at how shaky and un-abrupt my own conversion appeared to be in comparison. I wish I had known that not everyone experienced Jesus in this way.

Thomas, one of the disciples who walked alongside Jesus for months, experienced moments of doubt now infamous in the community of faith. In John 14, Jesus tells the disciples he is going to prepare a way for them and will come again. Thomas is the only one bold enough to ask the question, "Lord, we do not know where you are going. How can we know the way?" (v. 5). Jesus responds, "I am the way, and the truth, and the life. No one comes to the Father except through me" (v. 6).

Jesus uses Thomas and his doubts to clearly communicate his purpose and place, not only to the rest of his disciples, but eventually to the whole world. Yet after Jesus's death, Thomas is not with Mary Magdalene and the other disciples when Jesus appears to them, and he doubts their witness. "Unless I see in his hands the mark of the nails, and place my finger into the mark of the nails, and place my hand into his side, I will never believe" (John 20:25).

Oh how I relate to this doubting Thomas.

One week later, the Lord appears to Thomas. He shows him the wounds upon his hands and side and simply says, "Stop doubting and believe" (John 20:27b NIV). Thomas replies, "My Lord and my God!" (v. 28 NIV). After Pentecost, Thomas travels outside the Roman Empire to preach the Word of God and establish a church in India. He was likely the first person to bring the gospel to the Far East.

Like Paul and Thomas, the Lord made you and knows you intimately. His call on your heart has a unique purpose. For some, your call might come as a clap of thunder or a fast wind. For me, the Lord knew I needed, like Elijah (1 Kings 19) and like Samuel (1 Samuel 3), a still small voice.

THE JESUS I WANT YOU TO KNOW

We don't all have lightning bolt stories like Paul. But that doesn't make your conversion any less real or certain. Your hope was sealed by the Holy Spirit the moment you put your trust in Jesus as your Lord and Savior.

Maybe you accepted Jesus into your life and immediately turned from sin. Maybe he's working in and through your struggles at a much slower pace. No matter the outward appearance of your Christian identity, inner renewal is a life-long journey through the deepening knowledge of the character and Word of God (see Ephesians 4:22–24). It will undoubtedly include seasons of fear, struggle, and doubt, but as you seek him, he will continue to reveal himself to you.

Whether your conversion looks like Paul's (dramatic and sudden), or Thomas's (slow to develop and full of questions), or maybe somewhere in between—rest assured that the Lord has the same merciful love for you and will use your story for his glory.

DEVOTIONAL QUESTIONS

Read Ephesians 1:13.

1. Describe what it means to have your faith sealed with the Holy Spirit.

2. The author of chapter 20 describes feeling like her conversion story wasn't dramatic or exciting enough to be real. Can you relate?

3. If you feel unsure of the Spirit's seal over your heart, pray these words from Mark 9:24, "I believe; help my unbelief!"

NEW LIFE (noun): When Christ saves us, he transfers us from death and darkness into life and light. The joy and peace we experience as Christians is evidence of this transfer to new life.

What this means for you: You are no longer a slave to death—to your sin, shame, or the things of this world that pull you into a state of darkness. While you will always struggle with sin, you have the certainty of forgiveness and the hope of enjoying new life in Christ both now and forever.

Chapter 21
Idolatry and God's Pleasure
by Rebecca Lankford

On a sunny October day during my senior year, I sat anxiously in the crowded stands of the Mountain Brook High School gymnasium with one thing on my mind: Homecoming court election results. This was the Homecoming pep rally, an event I had been dreaming of for months on end; the time when I would learn if I would be named Homecoming Queen. The whole pep rally was a painful exercise in maintaining my composure, as each cheerleading routine and club presentation seemingly got slower by the minute. When the time finally came for the SGA president to announce the Homecoming court, my stomach churned in anticipation. *This*, I remember thinking, had the potential to be one of the happiest memories of my life—the kind I'd share with my grandchildren someday.

You probably know where this is going: the painful moment of truth arrived as I heard my name announced for Senior Homecoming court, indicating that I had not been elected Queen. While I should have been delighted to have the honor of being on the court at all, my heart sank in dissatisfaction. I faked a smile, accepted a bouquet of flowers, and watched as someone else was crowned Queen.

Why was my heart so set on being Homecoming Queen? Why was I so ungrateful and disappointed to be "second place" on the court? While the crown and the front cover of the school newspaper would have been a nice perk, I longed for the title because I craved affirmation; there was no greater feeling than knowing I was liked. Whether it was a "cool" kid laughing at a joke I told, or a teacher writing "nice work" on my paper, I relished every opportunity for affirmation. To be crowned Queen, in my mind, would have been the *ultimate* vindication that I was liked, admired, and adored. If admiration and delight were my ultimate destination, winning Homecoming Queen was my one-way ticket there.

When I found out I had been nominated for the Homecoming Court, I knew I was treading on dangerous ground. By the time I was a senior, I had enough self-awareness to realize I cared about how others perceived me. *A lot*. What I didn't realize, however, was how deeply this approval idol had lodged itself in my heart. I became enslaved to every source of earthly love, affirmation, and favor.

While I was already a Christian and cognitively *knew* that being Homecoming Queen wouldn't change my identity in Christ, my head and my heart had a hard time reconciling that truth. So, as Homecoming drew near, I tried my best to "act natural." I told myself and others I didn't care about the outcome, that I was just honored to be nominated at all.

This was a total lie. My craving to be Queen took over my life. I found myself being extra friendly in the hallways; I daydreamt in class about my reaction upon hearing my name announced at the pep rally; I spent hours looking for the *perfect* homecoming outfit (needs to go well with a crown!). Most embarrassingly, I would sit in class silently guessing who each of my classmates would vote for, tallying up my shot at success. While I tried to fight and pray against these impulses, my desire for a school-wide stamp of approval was too great. I was willing to give this idol just about anything it demanded of me.

I wish I could say that despite not being elected Queen, I still had a great Senior Homecoming. Unfortunately, our idols often rob us of the joy the Lord graciously offers in their place. I put on a happy face, but inside I was full of envy and disappointment. I had built a massive altar to the human approval idol, only to have it burned to ashes in a single afternoon. I had lost the thing I held most dear: the affirmation that I was liked, valued, and admired. Without the crown, I felt as if I had failed at my quiet but persistent mission of making sure everyone noticed me, approved of me, and delighted in me.

In hindsight, I'm now thankful to say that the disappointment of not being crowned Homecoming Queen was nothing but a gracious gift from the Lord. Had he given me the thing I most desired, it would have only intensified my approval addiction. I can only imagine how long I would have relished in my pride, never admitting that I was still massively insecure.

Perhaps standing in front of the school in a crown sounds like a nightmare to you. Maybe you *were* Homecoming Queen (or King!). No matter the case, deep within us all lies a hunger for approval and affirmation, an assurance that we are enough. This might look like a desperate longing for your dad to tell you "good job" after a game, for that cute guy to finally look your way in Chemistry class or, perhaps, just a friend telling you that they enjoy spending time with you.

The trouble with human approval, as with all idols, is its short expiration date. Where, then, do we find the lasting, secure, and satisfying approval which we so desperately crave? Only in Jesus, the One who came to show us what it *really* means to be loved. The gift of losing Homecoming Queen was my first step in finding Jesus—my truest source of affirmation, approval, and love.

THE JESUS I WISH I KNEW IN HIGH SCHOOL

When we are united to Christ by faith, we are sealed with an eternal stamp of approval and deep, steadfast *love*. The truth is, as a child of God, the Creator of heaven and earth is *well-pleased* with you.

God's pleasure with us isn't just a mushy platitude given to make us feel okay about ourselves. It is a biblical reality. After John the Baptist baptized Jesus, we read that "the Spirit [descended] on [Jesus] like a dove. And a voice came from heaven, 'You are my beloved Son; with you I am well pleased'" (Mark 1:10b–11). This passage makes it pretty clear how God feels about Jesus: he calls him *beloved*; God is *well-pleased* with him. In this moment, we see God bestowing his pleasure on Jesus simply because he is his Son.

Ephesians 1:5 tells us that God "predestined us for *adoption* to himself as sons through Jesus Christ," meaning that before we took our first breath, God wanted us in his family. As adopted children, God loves us the same way he loves his own Son Jesus. Colossians 3:3b says that our lives are "hidden with Christ." This means that when God looks at you, he not only sees you as the unique creation he made you to be, he also sees you covered—*hidden*—by the perfect life of his Son.

In the great exchange that happened on the cross, Jesus takes your sin, and you receive his righteousness and his Sonship. The way God feels about Jesus is the exact same way God feels about *you*: beloved and well-pleased. If you are in Christ, the Spirit of God's love and pleasure is resting on you just as it did with Jesus at his baptism. And it isn't going anywhere.

Romans 8:14–15 expands on this idea: "For all who are led by the Spirit of God are sons of God. For you did not receive the spirit of slavery to fall back into fear, but you have received the Spirit of adoption as sons, by whom we cry, 'Abba! Father!'" Our adoption declares us free from the "spirit of slavery" that leads to fear.

People pleasers often live with the fear of losing someone's approval or affirmation, believing the lie that if we are not valued by others, we are worthless. This line of thinking can make us "slaves" to the human approval idol, the same way I was a slave to becoming Homecoming Queen. But now, we have been given the very Spirit of God within us to continually reassure us of his boundless, steadfast, and eternal love.

The God who made heaven and earth looks upon you and me and he is *pleased*. He doesn't just put up with us, he *delights* in us. He loves spending time with us. He thinks we are a work of art. As funny as it sounds, Jesus is so happy that you and I belong to him that he *sings* over us (see Psalm 149:4 and Zephaniah 3:17).

There is great freedom in allowing this truth to change our hearts. Resting in God's favor means we can face criticism, nasty comments, bullies, even lost elections because we know that the God of the universe is *well-pleased* with us. Not only does he love you, he also really *likes* you. The favor of God is an eternal, heavenly favor that is far sweeter and more durable than any form of approval found on earth.

I wish I could go back and visit seventeen-year-old Rebecca on that sunny October day. I wish I could give her a big hug and tell her how much God delights in her, his beloved daughter. I wish I could help her believe that she did not need the bouquet, the crown, or the newspaper cover to be adored; she already had all the adoration she could ever need from her heavenly Father. I wish I could encourage her to live as a daughter, not a slave.

THE JESUS I WANT YOU TO KNOW

Reader, I want you to know that in Christ, you have the freedom to rest from your endless quest for approval. You can love others out of the kindness of Jesus, because in him, you already have the affirmation you so desperately crave. The next time you feel worthless, run to him and remember that he, the God who laid down his life for you, is well-pleased with you. Not because of what you've done, but because of what he has done to make you his child.

In Christ, you are an adopted child of God. You don't wear a flimsy plastic crown; you are crowned with *his* righteousness. You are not held captive by fear and approval; you are free to live and delight in his love.

DEVOTIONAL QUESTIONS

Read Ephesians 1:5–6.

1. How does God desire to relate to his people? Does he want to be far off from us or near? How near?

2. The author of chapter 21 describes her desire to be admired and accepted. Does the quest for human approval ever truly satisfy?

3. How might trusting in God's abounding love and approval change your life?

HIDDEN IN CHRIST (adjective): On the cross, Jesus was "clothed in our shame, crowned with our thorns, and exposed to the judgment of God that we deserve." On the cross, there was no place for Jesus to hide; he became our hiding place.

What this means for you: God passed all of his anger and judgment onto Jesus instead of you. In Christ, you have perfect peace and safety.

Chapter 22
Wounds and Restoration
by Peter Ong

I arrived in the United States at the age of five. My first few months in America, I spoke a few words: *yes, no,* and *I don't know.* We came to this country with literally forty-five dollars (my sister and I accidentally spent five of those dollars on the plane to watch a movie). Since we were so poor, I had to wear my sister's hand-me-downs. Yes, I wore pink overalls and blouses to school. In my first few weeks of school, I only had my Chinese name. So, when it came time for bathroom break, the class lined up in two lines, the boys and the girls. The teacher lined me up with the girls; I kept wanting to stand by the boys, but couldn't communicate to anyone that I was a boy. The teacher kept me on the girls' side.

As my teacher later recalled to me, when that first bathroom break was over, one of the girls told her, "He is a boy . . ." Teacher asked, "Why would you say that?" She responded, "He stands when he pees."

I was a child of Chinese immigrants and we had moved to a predominantly Italian, Irish, and German neighborhood in New York City's borough of Queens.

I was one of three Asian kids in our school, and looking back you would have thought we would have some sense of solidarity toward each other; but no, we were ashamed of each other.

We never spoke each other's names or looked each other in the eye. We saw the other as mirrors to our humiliation. We avoided each other with this fear that if we associated with one another, it would warrant an accumulated disdain. So we remained isolated in our individual injuries to our adolescent crime of being a foreigner.

I learned quickly that I was not welcome. The barbs were concise, short, and sharp:

Ching Chong

Chinese / Japanese / Dirty knees / Look at these / Chinese / Japanese / Dirty knees

Do you smell that? What? Smell . . .

It's Soy Sauce! Roast Pork. No. Roast Dog.

Slant-eyes.

These words felt more like pricks than trauma. They were things that passed through me like an emotional bruise. But what haunted me throughout the years of my childhood was their gaze. The glare of their eyes gave me a window into their internal scowl. Their offense and grimace when I spoke in class. My accent that I worked so hard to rid myself of.

Chinese / Japanese / Dirty knees / Look at these / Chinese / Japanese / Dirty knees

I could feel eyes all around me and while the words bruised, their looks felt like wounds that scarred. The glares from my classmates would proceed with cackles from mouths that synced with their eyes of passive contempt. Despite their effort to pretend that I didn't exist, my classmates made it clear that I had breached their spaces. In their whispers to each other, these refrains of exasperation escaped and I could measure their tone of disgust toward me through their pointed laughter.

I felt such deep shame and rage toward my own irreversible identity.

I remember one particularly painful experience when I was twelve. I was pummeled in a sandbox by several kids, including girls who threw sand at me while they taunted me. I ran home where my parents were mere shadows that appeared in and out

ᵣ as shells of humans that were exhausted by tedious
ɔmmutes and long days. I rarely engaged my parents, but
ᵣ our family traditions was to go to Chinatown on Sundays.
that Sunday I was still reeling from the experience in the
sandbox, and as we walked the littered streets to pick up gro-
ceries and eat, through tears I said to my father, "I hate Chinese
people, they are disgusting and dirty."

He looked at me with a sense of gravity. "I am Chinese, do
you hate me? Your mother is Chinese, do you hate her? *You* are
Chinese, do you hate yourself?" I sat there in silence with tears
unrelentingly covering my face.

That last question remained with me and it still haunts me.
"Do you hate yourself?"

Recently, I went to counseling, and one of the biggest discov-
eries and surprises that came out of it was learning that I was an
introvert at heart—meaning too much time around other people is
tiring. Those who know me might see me as anything but an introvert. I am usually gregarious and seen as energized by a crowd. But
through that counseling session, I learned that since childhood, I
had to be an extrovert to survive. I had to have a coping mecha-
nism, to be extroverted and outgoing in order to buffer some of
that pain of being a minority. It made so much sense to me.

THE JESUS I WISH I KNEW IN HIGH SCHOOL

"Do you hate yourself?"

This question from my father stays with me. It never completely goes away. Sometimes our internal voice is louder than
the external ones. We digest the shame and rejection and it mal-
nourishes our soul. It deforms and distorts our spiritual eyes with
the ability to see ourselves. That is why Scripture exhorts us with
Christ as the Light of the World. He is light in the darkness.
Looking to him as the light allows us to hold the tension that on
this side of heaven there will always be darkness as well as light.
Jesus knew firsthand of the brokenness of this world where the
weary and wandering are often afflicted with such a deep sense
of hatred and betrayal.

Christ reminds us in his life and death, *I occupied that space with you, in all that pain you went through. Every taunt, every marring of your dignity, every disregard you endured. If you hold on, behind it you will see is the presence of One who is working in ways you cannot see.*

My Asian identity is precisely how he made me, as Psalm 139 says, fearfully and wonderfully.

God used these very experiences in my life to give me the compassion to enter into the lives of those who are the most forgotten. God used my childhood hate for Chinatown to eventually love it and the Chinese church as an adult. God called me into ministry to immigrant kids in that very neighborhood, to teach them and also learn from their faith. God used my experience to give me a unique empathy to immigrant parents, because they were just like my parents. I wept with them because I saw my parents in them, as they struggled to provide for their kids in such a strange and unforgiving new country. Each day of my ministry as an adult, I am reminded of how God redeemed every broken moment in my teenage years to show me the other side of what seemed broken.

I remember one time in ministry in Chinatown, one of the elementary school kids yelled out, "God is Chinese!" I thought a joke was about to follow, so I waited. A pause. But this child nodded with affirmation. "It says that we are created in God's image and I am Chinese and he must look Chinese!" I was about to go into a theological explanation about God as Chinese, but I paused and thought, that is the beauty of the gospel. He has imprinted into our hearts that we are uniquely created in the image of God. God's love comes to us in a one-way, downward direction, and he did that by becoming one of us. He dwells in all the diversity of this humanity. And when he returns, I will declare in my Chinese tongue with my Spanish-speaking brethren, "Holy, Holy, Holy, is the Lord God Almighty," because he created us in his image. In all its beauty and redeemed brokenness.

God was using that time not as a way of giving me pain, but to prepare my heart, that I would know he was with me the whole time. He didn't just see the fractures I faced but empathized as he entered into this broken world as Isaiah prophesied, "In all their affliction he was afflicted" (Isaiah 63:9a). And, "the LORD . . . anointed [Christ] to bring good news to the poor . . . to bind up the brokenhearted . . . to comfort all who mourn" (61:1–2). God was so close, and I could go to Christ because as a part of his rescue mission, he took on flesh and was also, like me, afflicted.

Christ traveled downward in pursuit of rescuing us, not only to deal with our sin but also to be Emmanuel—which means "God with Us"—in the midst of our pain and weariness. He knew the implications of our shame and troubled hearts. He came into the world as the agonizing Shepherd facing the cross. As he went to cross, he experienced the full measure of our despair and yet responded with the full measure of his love to comfort us. He gathered us as the rejected, for we have a Sovereign who was rejected by the very people he sought to rescue. And on the cross, he experienced the cosmic rejection of his very own Father (see Mark 15:34).

When we cry out to God and lament, "You don't understand and you don't care," we are met by a God who *does* understand, and who cared for us so much that he went to be abandoned. He did all of this so that we would never be abandoned by the One who went to the depths for us.

THE JESUS I WANT YOU TO KNOW

My friend, the overarching declaration of God for all the loss you experience is *resurrection*. For every death set before you, there is a declaration that Christ is the Resurrection and the Life. There is beauty for ashes. There is life after death. For everything that has been lost there is still another chapter that God is telling through it—and that chapter is one of unfolding renewal. That renewal will be precisely unique to you and your pain and your story. He is not far, rather he is so intimately close. Listen to the Holy Spirit testify in your heart that you are a child of his.

Whenever you struggle with this idea of why God made you the way you are—and those creeping thoughts invade your heart, you can trust that *my God stays*. He desires to be the lifter of your head (see Psalm 3:3). He wants you to meet his gaze with the fullness and assurance that you are his and he is yours. He is saying, "I am your Abba. I see you and love you. And in all these broken pieces of yours, I will make a mosaic of such beauty. Just hold on and I will show you."

Devotional Questions
Read Psalm 139.

1. Have you ever felt like an outsider? What was the setting? How did others treat you, and how did you feel in response? Can you identify with the author's question, "Do you hate yourself?"
2. How does Psalm 139 describe God's view of you?
3. How might God already be using some of your most painful experiences for his glory—as a part of your developing story—a story he knew and planned from the beginning?

REDEMPTION (noun): In the Bible, redemption refers to crossing over from one thing to another. When Jesus redeems a person, he alters them from darkness to light, from death to life, from an enemy of God to a child of God, from judgment to eternal life.

What this means for you: In Christ, you are walking this earth as a redeemed person—one who was once dead, but now has the promise of new life in Christ. Once you were lost, but now you are found. At this moment you are fully redeemed, and yet still *being* redeemed. Christ is *right now* in the process of making all things new.

Chapter 23
Weariness and the Kingdom
by Liz Edrington

The electric red numbers on my alarm clock blinked, "1:15 a.m."

Seriously? I thought to myself.

We'd returned late from an away soccer game and I still hadn't showered, wanting to get through my AP French homework and start studying for my AP World History test as quickly as possible.

Sitting cross-legged in the middle of my bed, which was more like a nest of notes and timelines, I rubbed my face and took stock of the grass stains splashed across my soccer jersey.

My body ached, and my brain felt full-to-the-brim with information I was sure I'd never remember. I needed at least another half-hour of studying.

I had it in my head that if I just worked hard enough to get into a good college and hopefully pick up a scholarship or two along the way, *then* I could rest. I could get away from my parents' endless fighting about not having enough money. I could figure out who I was apart from constantly trying to help their failing marriage and encourage my struggling older brother.

My future was up to me. My rest was up to me. Creating peace in my family was up to me. Without realizing it, I had made myself the king of my own world.

I looked up. The quote on my ceiling, sometimes attributed to Mother Teresa, reminded me of this weight: "I know God won't give me anything I can't handle. I just wish he didn't trust me so much."

The part of me that liked being the king of my own universe felt a sense of accomplishment in considering all that I was getting done—the homework, the babysitting, the refereeing, the Young Life leading, the student athletic training, and sports during all seasons. But the flip side of that was the fear that my kingdom would fall apart if I took my eye off the ball. If I let something slip, if I failed, a deep part of me believed that my world would unravel. It was up to me to hold everything together.

On the outside, I was the positive encourager who sought to be the good teammate, friend, student, and daughter. I was a fair and hardworking king when it came to my kingdom.

But on the inside, I was never content with anything I'd done. I rarely paused to check in with myself; if I would have, I'd have discovered that I was exhausted. And I wasn't actually sure I liked that God trusted me as much as he did. It was a lot of pressure. I was weary. The Lord always had something else he needed me to do.

I remember wondering, *Will this ever end?* I especially felt this way when I hadn't studied enough, hadn't managed to stop my parents' fighting, or hadn't done a good enough job sharing Jesus with my peers.

I couldn't imagine life being different, and the responsibility I felt to make it different was beyond overwhelming. A part of me wanted to step down from this throne, but I felt pressure to continue.

It was up to me.

THE JESUS I WISH I KNEW IN HIGH SCHOOL

"You do you" seems like an encouraging, non-judgmental statement, doesn't it? "Live your truth" sounds like a freeing banner under which we can all live peacefully as individuals.

But what about when your truth doesn't actually set you free? What about when "doing you" turns out to be enslaving, because "doing you" means striving for a moving target that is always out of reach?

These mantras sound good, but they don't deliver the freedom and security they proclaim.

Had they been around when I was in high school, they would have fed into the over-responsibility I felt for my family, my future, and my friendships. They would have affirmed the various types of perfection-striving tendencies that were at work in my life (such as academics, athletics, and beauty). They would have supported the sense that my identity, purpose, and happiness were up to me.

In my life, "living my truth" created an enormous amount of stress and pressure. It created an endless cycle of trying to earn my rest and prove my worth. There was always more to do, and my doing was never enough. I was living as the king of my own world.

At this point in my life, I knew Jesus as a good friend who was helping me to survive. He was kind, he was loyal, and he loved me in spite of my flaws. But he also trusted me with way more than I felt like I could handle. In actuality, I longed for direction and protection from someone other than myself.

Colossians 1:16–18 says:

> For by him all things were created, in heaven and on earth, visible and invisible, whether thrones or dominions or rulers or authorities—all things were created through him and for him. And he is before all things, and in him all things hold together. And he is the head of the body, the church. He is the beginning, the firstborn from the dead, that in everything he might be preeminent.

This doesn't sound like the little Jesus I had on call when needed. This sounds like a King who is powerful enough to both create and destroy, who is holding the whole universe together. This sounds like a Ruler who is much less interested in how much he can entrust in me, and far more interested that *I* trust *him*.

Knowing Jesus as King would have changed how I related to the world. It would have helped me realize that the weight of God's kingdom did not fall on my shoulders. I would have been more honest about what was hard and broken in my life, instead of constantly trying to convince myself of what I could handle. I would have found hope in God's promise to use all things for his glory (Romans 8:28)—meaning not just my successes and gifts, but my sorrow, weaknesses, disappointments, and failures as well.

For those of us who don't live under a monarchy, it can be hard to envision what life under the protection and blessing of our true King is like. All comparison fails, because it cannot accurately represent our perfectly loving and good God. But I think it might be similar to playing for the best coach you could ever imagine.

When I was in high school, my field hockey coach was a big part of my life. Coach Lee was a no-nonsense woman who had a voice that could cut through a crowd. Chatter would stop when she walked into the locker room, because we respected her and wanted to hear what she had to say. We feared and revered her, but we also knew she was so utterly *for us*. We trusted her leadership, knowing she would take us further than we imagined we could go. She knew what we could become, and she invited us to follow her in the journey of getting there.

To understand what it would be like with Jesus "ruling" as King or coach, we have to use our imaginations. We would delight in playing for him simply because of how amazing he was, and we would thrive under his guidance. He would know the rules far better than we did (he invented the game after all), so he'd continually be teaching us about the art of playing. We'd hang on his every word. We would have so much fun discovering new techniques and tactics of the game!

Unlike a human coach/ruler, though, Jesus never lets us down. He is no mere influencer or role model: He is Lord. And his ultimate priority is always love. He is honest about our strengths and weaknesses and reminds us that we are valuable members of the team (his family)—not because of our skill or achievements, but because we are his. He doesn't need for us to win, for he has already secured the win (defeating sin and the enemy of darkness) through his death and resurrection.

So what's left when you've already got the win?

The best part is left.

We get to live and learn and love as King Jesus's beloved children. We get to spend our lives discovering how to play and enjoy the game (life in his kingdom) to his glory and not our own. We get to trust the only One who has ever been perfectly trustworthy instead of trusting our own shifting emotions.

One of the most life-changing things I've learned since high school is that Christ is not only my friend: he is my King. And he is currently reigning on his throne. Life under King Jesus isn't a constant proving: it's the unfathomable one-way grace of Jesus. And being a member of his team—citizen of his kingdom—means that I am utterly secure.

Instead of living "my truth," I am living God's truth—a story much larger than myself. Here, I am invited to rest in the knowledge that Christ delights in using every little thing—my failures and successes, my faith and my doubts—for his glory's sake. Here, I can breathe. I am learning to trust him with more of my life as I discover the many, beautiful, mysterious ways his kingdom is at work.

THE JESUS I WANT YOU TO KNOW

Friend, here is what I want you to know: there is rest for you in King Jesus. Your place in his kingdom isn't dependent on you or on anything you've done (or not done); it is dependent on his finished work on the cross. Your contributions are welcome and they make an impact, but they aren't needed to sustain the kingdom.

There is such freedom in being a part of his kingdom: it isn't one that has to be created, maintained, or advertised by you. Your belonging is an objective truth, secured through Christ. You get to come as you are and behold the way the Lord loves to reveal himself in and through all parts of your story. You get to study for your tests, honor your teammates, and serve your friends, not to earn or prove your worth but to worship the One who delights in revealing himself through you.

When you realize you have become king over a part of your life—be that your academics, your sexuality, your athletics, or something else—I invite you to step off your throne and put that piece of your life back under the authority of the King. This is repentance. What relief it brings to trust Jesus with these things instead of trying to control them ourselves. Before you get out of bed each morning, know that King Jesus delights in the most basic and fundamental truth that you are his. You belong to him.

DEVOTIONAL QUESTIONS

Read Colossians 1:16–18.

1. What does this passage teach you about Jesus?
2. The author of chapter 23 describes her tendency to be the king of her own kingdom, and to control all aspects of her life. How can you relate? How does ruling your own life leave you feeling at the end of the day?
3. What would it be like to hand over the small and large details of your life to mighty King Jesus, and to trust him as your good and loving Shepherd?

THE LAW (noun): The law often refers to God's commandments in the Bible. We can understand it as God's blueprints for human flourishing. Instead of trusting Jesus with our identity and worth, we often look to law-following to justify ourselves. But the law cannot give us life; the Holy Spirit is the One who gives us life.

What this means for you: Because of Jesus, you no longer live under the law; you live *in the Spirit*. While the law is good, your fallen nature makes it impossible to follow every command perfectly. If it were possible, Jesus would not have needed to live a perfect life and die a criminal's death on your behalf. Because of Jesus, your inability to live perfectly is not counted against you, and your good behavior does not gain extra favor. There is nothing you can do to make God love you more, and there is nothing you can do to make God love you less. He loves you perfectly and completely.

Chapter 24
Secrets and Mercy
by Davis Lacey

I worked hard to project a certain image during my high school days. As a prototypical Enneagram-3 ("Achiever"), it wasn't enough for me to *be* successful in as many endeavors as possible. I needed people to *see* just how wonderful and successful I was.

In academics, I was our school's valedictorian. In athletics, I earned my black belt in tae kwon do. As a Boy Scout, I became an Eagle Scout. And as a musician, I was selected for All-State Band all four years of high school. I did all of these activities while faithfully attending church services, taking on leadership roles in my youth group, and serving as a student chaplain for a few of the aforementioned organizations. I wanted to be perceived as a *successful* Christian, just as I wanted a successful reputation in my extracurricular pursuits.

While working tirelessly to maintain my daytime image, I was drawn to another image at night—a projected image on the screen of my internet-accessible iPod Touch. At first, I was simply dipping my toes in the ocean of internet pornography. Then, in what seemed like the blink of an eye, I found myself figuratively swimming in waters too deep to fathom.

Anyone who is secretly wrestling with any sort of addiction can relate to what came next: ongoing tidal waves of shame, remorse, and guilt that cascaded every time I failed to resist porn's allure. Worst of all was the feeling that I was letting Jesus down—partly because I had a sincere love for him, but mostly because I had no concept of a Savior who related to me differently than my instructors, Scoutmasters, and band directors.

A lackluster performance in music would surely result in me missing out on another All-State selection; why would my "performance" for Jesus work differently?

I was scared to death that my lack of success in fighting this temptation put me at risk of being demoted from Christ's graces. I doubted that Jesus could truly love a failure like me; the best I could hope for was that he tolerated me with disgust or with cold indifference. Having resigned myself to the reality that I could never be truly pleasing to Jesus, I focused on the next best thing: maintaining the charade of my public respectability so as to keep the admiration of my family and friends.

I went to great lengths to hide my pornography usage. I didn't do this because I thought I could beat my addiction, or because I enjoyed the constant presence of shame and self-loathing. Rather, I had a vision in my mind of what "coming clean" would look like: shock, repulsion, and condemnation. I couldn't stand the thought of my pastor, parents, teachers, or friends seeing me in the same way that I envisioned Jesus seeing me: as a hypocritical, un-lovable failure.

The All-American Rejects' song "Dirty Little Secret" was popular during my high school years. The lyrics describe perfectly my daily fight to cover up my own dirty little secret: "These sleeping dogs won't lie, and all I've tried to hide, it's eating me apart . . ."[1]

How I wish I knew then the Jesus I know now.

THE JESUS I WISH I KNEW IN HIGH SCHOOL

The words of John 10:14–15 were instrumental in giving me eventual victory in my fight against internet pornography, and

---

1. The All-American Rejects, "Dirty Little Secret," *Move Along* (Toledo: Doghouse Records, 2005), https://allamericanrejects.com/discography/move-along.

they continue to be the basis for my growth in the areas of vulnerability, transparency, and authenticity. There, Jesus says, "I am the good shepherd. I know my own and my own know me, just as the Father knows me and I know the Father; and I lay down my life for the sheep."

What is Jesus saying in these verses?

First, Jesus is saying that he knows his people better than they know themselves. Jesus says that he knows his people "just as" God the Father knows him, and "just as" he knows God the Father. The Father and Son so intimately know and share one another's attributes, plans, and purposes that they are described as being "one" (see John 10:30).

Jesus knows us with the same degree of intimacy. No sin is concealed, no fallen desire undetected, and no brokenness remains hidden from his gaze.

I grasped this truth in high school. Up to this point in time, however, I had wrongly assumed that Jesus was disgusted by me on account of what he saw. Just out of my view was a second theological truth found in the words of John 10:14–15—a truth which eventually led me out of hiding and into the grace-filled embrace of my Savior Jesus.

That second truth is this: Jesus is not like my instructors, band directors, or Scoutmasters. He does not deal with me based on my performance. The failures that drove me to run *from* Jesus are the very things that drive Jesus to run *toward* me.

What is Jesus's reaction to knowing me as intimately as he knows the Father? What is his response to my brokenness? The closing words of John 10:15 hold the answer: "I lay down my life for the sheep." Whereas Jesus had every reason to side against me on account of my sin, the cross of Christ is proof that my Savior has sided *against* my sin—but *with* me!

Far from issuing his wrath against me, my dirty little secret evokes my Savior's deepest sympathy, compassion, mercy, and grace. They are the very things which drew him out of heaven—to live the sinless life of righteousness I could not achieve, to lay down his life in order to pay the debt of my sinfulness, and to forever disarm sin and death by rising from the grave. Now, Jesus welcomes me to share his resurrection (Romans 6:5), which means that the following are true of me.

First, my shame is gone. Romans 10:11 says, "Everyone who believes in [Jesus] will not be put to shame." As one who shares in Christ's resurrection, I no longer have grounds to feel ashamed; Jesus willingly took my shame as his own (see 15:3). When he died, my grounds for shame died with him. When he was buried, so too was my shame. Now risen and living, shame has no claim on Jesus. And because I am one with him, shame has no claim on me, either. "There is therefore now no condemnation for those who are in Christ Jesus" (8:1).

Second, the love of Jesus is mine. Sharing Jesus's resurrection does more than simply remove my shame. Sharing Jesus's resurrection means that I am one with Jesus—to the point that the very love which the Father lavished on Jesus is lavished upon me as well (see John 17:26). Regardless of what my family, friends, etc. think about me, I could not possibly be more loved and affirmed. I am hidden in Christ, which means that God the Father loves me to the same degree that he loves Christ himself.

Third, healing is possible—through community. There were two main reasons that I did not reach out to others and ask for help dealing with pornography: I feared their shame-inducing reactions, and I feared losing their love/admiration/respect. The gospel alone gave me courage to confess my sins and to ask for help, because the gospel alone assured me that Christ had freed me from shame, and that his love would never depart from me. By the mercy of God, the friends to whom I confessed did not shame me, but affirmed me in my relationship with Christ. There's no shame in having a dire need for Jesus; it's the very reason he lived, died, and rose again. I'm thankful for the friends who heard my confession in this light—who allowed me to come out of the shadows and to experience the joy of Proverbs 27:17, "Iron sharpens iron, and one man sharpens another." My healing has taken place in the context of community.

How I wish I would have grasped these realities during my high school years! How I long for you to grasp them now—to know the love of your Savior, to have your brokenness healed, and to have the burden of your own secrets lifted from your shoulders.

THE JESUS I WANT YOU TO KNOW

Are you fighting tooth and nail to keep your own secret hidden? Are you shackled by the same feelings of shame, isolation, and condemnation which were once my daily companions? Dear reader: remember that the areas of your life in which your sin is most manifest are the same areas to which Christ's compassion is most mercifully supplied. Don't let your sin and your shame drive you from Jesus—because your dirty little secret is what first drove Jesus to you.

The life of Jesus has won for you a track record of perfect righteousness. The death of Jesus has forever cleansed the blemishes of your sinfulness. The resurrection of Jesus unites you with him forever, and secures for you the very same love and approval which God the Father shows to Christ himself. You could not possibly be more loved, accepted, or affirmed, and the reactions of other people will not change that reality.

You have everything you need to come out of hiding.

DEVOTIONAL QUESTIONS

Read Romans 10:11.

1. According to this Scripture, all who believe in Jesus will not be put to shame. Can you imagine the freedom of never experiencing shame again?

2. The author of chapter 24 describes his secret struggle with pornography. What sin or struggle have you kept hidden from others?

3. The grace we have in Jesus gives us the freedom to bring all of our sin and shame into the light. Who in

your life might speak words of grace and forgiveness over you, as you share your secret shame?

FREEDOM (noun): Being released from eternal death, bondage to sin, and the need to prove ourselves.

What this means for you: Freedom means that you can live like you've been forgiven. You can live like you are loved. You can dance like nobody's watching; you can wear that outfit you aren't so sure about; you can eat that ice cream that will bring you joy; you can let harsh words roll off your shoulders; you can live a big and ordinary and abundant life.

Chapter 25
Rebellion and God's Pursuit
by Chelsea Kingston Erickson

God called me to trust in him when I was just three years old, but I didn't really begin to understand his grace until I was seventeen.

Don't get me wrong—I loved Jesus as a teenager. In the midst of high school heartaches and often tumultuous relationships with my parents, he was my refuge. But somewhere, somehow, I believed the lie that I had to be *good* in order to stay close to him, that my relationship with him was based on how well I was performing in my faith.

Essentially, this motivated me to work *really hard* at hiding my sin—and even harder at achieving the image of the perfect Christian kid. (You know, the one who never misses a day of reading her Bible, has all the right Sunday school answers, and faithfully serves her church.) I loved the moments when I felt close to God. And I enjoyed the praise I received from my parents and other Christian adults in my life for my efforts to follow Jesus; I threw myself into all kinds of activities in search of this affirmation. But whenever I failed either to hide my sin or to perform in these ways, my self-esteem plummeted. I pictured myself being pushed farther and farther away from God.

Still, something in me didn't *want* to play the part of the good girl—at least, not all the time. The image I was trying to maintain was exhausting, and deep down I wanted to be liked by my peers too. I especially craved attention from boys, and I learned to get it: by being just the right mix of innocent and flirtatious.

My shallow understanding of God's love led me to live a double life. I was genuinely interested in growing closer to Jesus, but I suspected that this was only possible by self-effort. Meanwhile, I also loved the thrill of being just a little rebellious—of lying to my parents about where I was going, of driving my car just a little recklessly on the open roads of central Illinois farm country, and of making out with my on-again-off-again boyfriend.

Both of these approaches—my endless performance-oriented activities and my frenzied attention-seeking—became ways for me to feel valuable.

The only problem was, neither approach reliably "worked" for me. The approval of others was my drug. So whenever my boyfriend and I were on a break, or my parents and I were fighting, or I didn't get the attention I craved, I began to spiral emotionally. My unhealthy dependence on the approval of others led me to run from the reality of God's approval.

Dark thoughts gradually crept into my mind, and instead of banishing them with the truth of God's Word, I indulged them. I began to imagine how good it would feel to escape my constant need for affirmation. I began imagining what it would feel like to escape life all together.

Finally, in a moment of desperation, I gave into the darkness and tried ending my own life.

Under the bright fluorescent lights of the emergency room, as doctors worked to heal what I had broken, a strange calm washed over me. It was the comforting realization that God was *with me,* even in my very worst moment. I recalled the words of Psalm 139, which I had memorized in middle school: "Where shall I go from your Spirit? Or where shall I flee from your presence? . . . If I say, 'Surely the darkness shall cover me, and the light about me be night,' even the darkness is not dark to you" (vv. 7, 11–12a).

In the midst of the most shameful night of my life, I suddenly experienced the reality of those words: God had not abandoned me, even while I was running away. And for the first time, I realized that this was a gift, not something I had earned from him. In the darkest hour of my rebellion, he drew near, assuring me of his abundant love and presence.

THE JESUS I WISH I KNEW IN HIGH SCHOOL

In the years that followed, I found myself in church communities where the gospel of grace was preached regularly. I began to learn from God's Word what I had already experienced: that God's grace for me wasn't *only* for salvation; it was for my entire future. His sacrifice on the cross was enough to cover all of my sin and shame. There was nothing I could do, no performance I could offer, that could add to what he had already done. And even in my worst sin, there was no way I could out-run his love for me.

This freed me to live in a whole new way. Slowly, there were steps toward reconciliation with my parents, a change of heart in my relationships with boys, and a genuine desire to love and serve the Lord. Perhaps most miraculously, God provided release from the dark thoughts with which I had so often struggled. The transformation wasn't quick. In fact, it continues to this day. But God took my hard, divided heart and began to make it new (see Ezekiel 36:26).

John's gospel tells the story of a man named Nicodemus who, like me, found himself living a double life.

Nicodemus was a high-ranking member of the Jewish teaching class known as the Pharisees. These men were serious about studying the Jewish Scriptures (our Old Testament) and about watching for the Messiah, whom the prophets had promised. They expected the Messiah to liberate them from the Roman Empire and to inaugurate a political kingdom that would restore Israel to glory. For many of them, Jesus didn't fit this image.

Nicodemus found validation in his popular friends and his position, striving for excellence as one of Israel's teachers. The name *Nicodemus* means victory of the people. It resembles the modern brand name *Nike*. As my church's senior pastor has explained, Nicodemus was the "Just-Do-It Man!" He imagined he could save himself by his own efforts and achievement.

On the other hand, Nicodemus was deeply curious about this Jesus who claimed to be the Jewish Messiah. But in order to preserve his status, Nicodemus only went to Jesus under the cover of night, when he wouldn't be seen by his fellow Pharisees.

Jesus knew Nicodemus's heart, just as he knows yours and mine. In John 3, Nicodemus tried to prove all that he knew about the Scriptures, but Jesus said to him, "The wind blows where it wishes, and you hear its sound, but you do not know where it comes from or where it goes. So it is with everyone who is born of the Spirit" (v. 8). Jesus was saying that in order to be saved, Nicodemus must first experience God's grace—something that is completely and entirely free. It's something that Nicodemus couldn't buy and something that he couldn't control. Jesus told Nicodemus that in order to enter the kingdom of God, he must be born again. In other words, he must have a new heart.

Although Nicodemus didn't initially accept Jesus's invitation to new life, he *was* different. In John 7, we read that when some of the Jewish leaders were looking for a way to kill Jesus, Nicodemus spoke up. While he wasn't quite ready to declare allegiance to Jesus—he also wasn't willing to subject him to unfair treatment.

Nicodemus is mentioned once more in John's gospel, when he provided a lavish offering to anoint Jesus's body for burial. Maybe John included this snapshot to reassure us that Nicodemus's heart truly had been changed: he had finally come to realize that he couldn't "Just Do It." His costly demonstration of honor for Jesus leads us to believe that Nicodemus had come to see his own need for God's grace.

Like me, Nicodemus tried to get to God on his own terms, but found that his efforts didn't work. He wanted a little bit of

Jesus, and all the approval of his peers, too. His divided heart led him to hide parts of his life from others until Jesus finally captured his whole heart.

Soon after that day in the hospital when God captured my heart by grace, I read this quote, which resonates with trying to get to God on my own terms:

> So long as we imagine that it is we who have to look for God, then we must often lose heart. But it is the other way about: he is looking for us. And so we can afford to recognize that very often we are not looking for God; far from it, we are in full flight from him, in high rebellion against him. And he knows that and has taken it into account. He has followed us into our own darkness; there where we thought finally to escape him, we run straight into his arms. So we do not have to erect a false piety for ourselves, to give us the hope of salvation. Our hope is in his determination to save us. And he will not give in![1]

THE JESUS I WANT YOU TO KNOW

Friend, this is the gospel I want you to know: God loves you so fiercely, and he is looking for you (even when you are on the run from him).

There is nothing you can do to prove yourself or earn your way to him, and there is nothing you can do to out-sin his grace. My choice to try to harm myself was a foolish one, and oh how I pray that you will learn from my mistakes. When you are tempted to run away, may you run to the God of grace instead.

Our God has followed us into our darkest places by sending his beloved Son. Jesus did what we could never do by living the perfect life and dying the death we deserve. He has become the true victory by triumphing over sin and death forever. My

---

1. Simon Tugwell, *Prayer: Living with God* (Springfield: Templegate, 1975), 52.

prayer is that you will give him your whole heart and whole life, resting in the grace of the gospel.

DEVOTIONAL QUESTIONS
Read John 3:1–17.

1. Do you share any connections with Nicodemus? How might Jesus's words to Nicodemus comfort your own heart?

2. The author of chapter 25 describes living a double life. What are some secret or hidden parts of your life that you need to bring into the light before God?

3. How does God's grace enable you to bring your whole life before God?

TRANSFORMATION (OR SANCTIFICATION)

(nouns): The process whereby a Christian grows in dependence on the grace of God. As they depend on God, the Lord changes them into a more Christlike person, although they will continue to struggle with sin.

What this means for you: No matter how long you walk with the Lord, you will always still be a sinner. But as you look more and more to Jesus for your rescue, over time you will become more like him. This is God's grace, and nothing of your own doing.

Chapter 26
Imperfect Parents and God's Family
by Anna Meade Harris

Now I lay me down to sleep . . .
   Every night during my growing-up years, my family would pray together. My parents and younger brother and I would come together for a minute or two to repeat this prayer I'd heard all my life.

> I pray the Lord my soul to keep.
> If I should die before I wake,
> I pray the Lord my soul to take.

After that familiar bit, we prayed for God to bless a long list of relatives. We did this every single night for the first eighteen years of my life.

And then after the final *Amen*, all hell would break loose.

Most nights, my parents fought. Loud and long and mean and scary. There were many nights when prayer time was effectively just a pause button in the middle of the yelling. Compounding the conflict was the fact that one parent drank too much and the other parent didn't drink at all. They didn't seem to agree about anything. As a child, I didn't understand why they picked at each other so much. They often seemed to be searching for the meanest, most hurtful retorts they could find, like they were in an insult contest and someone would eventually win. But of course, all four of us lost every single fight.

My brother and I had roles in the daily drama. He was two and a half years younger than me, cute and funny and personable. When the arguments started, he would slip away to his room to find refuge in his record collection and video games. He was brilliant at turning up the volume to tune out the turmoil. I turned to books for comfort, but the problem with reading is that you can still hear the yelling down the hall.

I was also hampered by an urgent sense that I had to do something about the fighting. I don't remember ever consciously thinking the fights were my fault, but I was very careful to be good so my parents could never have cause to argue about me. Instead, I felt responsible to do what I could to make peace between them; in fact, I somehow read the Bible to mean that I was *supposed* to fix their relationship. There were a couple of Bible verses that I misapplied to our situation. The first, of course, was the fifth commandment: "honor your father and mother" (Exodus 20:12a). The other worked in tandem: "blessed are the peacemakers" (Matthew 5:9a). That verse became my battle cry. Whenever I went to intervene in the fights, I reminded myself, "blessed are the peacemakers," and dove headfirst into trying to make that peace.

I mediated the arguing in lots of ways. Sometimes I walked right into the fight, tried to get them to settle down, and coached them to speak rationally and kindly to each other. Other times I waited until the next day, finding a calmer moment to invite one or the other of them to tell me their side of last night's battle. I even wrote down what I thought could be solutions to their problems. I first gave my parents a suggested budget when I was eight years old. The first item on my list was cutting out our weekly trip to the gas station for candy; the fourth item on the list—placed strategically so that they wouldn't think it was a big deal—was eliminating alcohol.

The worst fights happened after midnight. When I sensed one of these brewing, I could not fall asleep—afraid that if I didn't wake up and intervene, my dad might be gone in the morning. In the middle of the night I could hear him through my bedroom wall, grabbing his suitcase to pack and leave. That banging around in his closet was always my cue to get out of bed, knock on their bedroom door, and turn on the tears. I would plead with them to be quiet so they wouldn't wake my brother, then I'd feign surprise at the sight of the packed suitcase. I always begged my dad to sleep on the couch downstairs rather than leave. I don't know what I thought would happen if he left, I only knew that the thought of his driving away into the night was terrifying.

One night when I was about sixteen, something shifted inside me. I numbly got up from my bed to try to stop the fight, but I couldn't make myself cry. I just stood and watched my mom cry while my dad packed. When he waited for me to beg him to stay, I said, "Leave if you need to." I went back to my room and went to bed.

I wish I could say that night was the last time I tried to fix my parents. It wasn't. But it was my first glimpse of freedom from the burden of carrying my family on my back. By the grace of God, I simply ran out of ideas and energy, and for the moment, I let go.

THE JESUS I WISH I KNEW IN HIGH SCHOOL

I had never told anyone about the fighting at home because I thought that would dishonor my parents, but I was desperate in so many ways. Teetering on the edge of an eating disorder, failing math, and fighting insomnia had me worn out. Of course the chaos at home didn't cause all those problems, but I couldn't risk adding to my parents' list of reasons to fight. I reached the end of myself and called my pastor.

The things my pastor shared with me corrected my misunderstanding of those Bible verses. He gave me a much deeper understanding of Jesus's work on the cross and his will for me in my earthly family.

First, he assured me that confiding in him was not dishonoring my parents. Rather than broadcasting their troubles to nosy neighbors, I came for counsel to the very counselor God had provided for me. He began to teach me that in Christ, I had been adopted into the family of God. When Jesus said that "whoever does the will of my Father in heaven is my brother and sister and mother," he wasn't saying that our earthly parents aren't important (see Matthew 12:50). That fifth commandment still stands. What he is saying is that the family he has created for us in the body of Christ, in his church, is where our truest, deepest fellowship will be found. The church is his provision for us that supersedes the biological family we were born into, and when those earthly families let us down—as his did, as yours and mine will—the church is designed to help us. We were never meant to fight our battles alone. In coming to my pastor for help, I was participating in that larger family that, in Christ, God had brought me in to.

My pastor spoke with deep compassion for my parents and their struggles. Just as I couldn't fix my insomnia or my eating issues with my own willpower or determination, neither could my parents stop fighting even though they knew they should (see Romans 7:15). If I couldn't fix myself, why did I think I could fix my parents? That was something Jesus never meant for me to do. It was never my responsibility to mend their relationship. That was Jesus's job, and he was the only one who could ever right what was wrong between them. Jesus gave me tools to live in peace in the middle of all the fighting: he gave me Scripture, prayer, and my larger church family. But he did not give me the tools to fix my parents.

Jesus lived for us, died for us, and rose again from the dead, all to do for us what we cannot do for ourselves or for the ones we love. Just as I need a Savior, so do my parents, and I can never be that savior for them. I am responsible to pray for them, and that is all the burden I can possibly carry. "Cast your burden on the Lord, and he will sustain you" (Psalm 55:22a).

I'll admit, once I began to feel less responsible for my parents, I realized I was pretty mad that I had ever felt responsible in the first place. In fact, I felt that way for years. But God has used this to teach me too. He has poured out so much grace on me that I have grown eager to forgive as I have been forgiven, through the finished work of Jesus on the cross (see Colossians 3:13).

THE JESUS I WANT YOU TO KNOW

If you, my friend, find yourself in a home that feels more like a war zone than a welcome haven, please know that the problems there are not yours to fix. Everyone in every home is broken by the effects of sin. You cannot make your loved ones submit to God for guidance and healing, but with his help, you can learn to love and trust God yourself. And if someone who is supposed to take care of you lets you down or leaves, God promises he never will: "I WILL NEVER [under any circumstances] DESERT YOU [nor give you up nor leave you without support, nor will I in any degree leave you helpless], NOR WILL I FORSAKE or LET YOU DOWN or RELAX MY HOLD ON YOU [assuredly not]!" (Hebrews 13:5b AMP).

I wish I could tell you that the gospel has freed me completely, but I still have a stubborn heart. I still try to fix my parents from time to time. My church family is good about reminding me that only Jesus can change any of us. My hope for my parents, and for myself, is in Jesus alone. He (not me) is doing a new thing, in my heart and in the hearts of my parents. Jesus makes a way in the wilderness and streams in the wasteland, and—praise him—I don't have to do any of that. And neither do you (see Isaiah 43:19).

DEVOTIONAL QUESTIONS

Read Matthew 12:50.

1. Jesus says that our true family is found in the body of Christ. How have you seen your church or youth group take on the role of family in your life?
2. The author of chapter 26 describes her desire to fix and control the broken parts of her family. In what ways do

you see yourself trying to fix and control areas of your own life?

3. What would it look like for you to surrender your heart—and your attempts to be in control—to Jesus? Can you trust him to do the fixing?

THE BODY OF CHRIST (noun): This is the worldwide church, Christ's hands and feet on earth—you, me, and our various local churches and Christian organizations.

What this means for you: As a Christian, you are a member of the body of Christ. Whether you know it or not, you bring Jesus with you wherever you go, to whomever you are with. Similarly, the body of Christ you surround yourself with is a powerful support—a wellspring of Jesus and the gospel in your own life.

Chapter 27
Blame and the Great Exchange
by Kenneth E. Ortiz

My parents weren't believers, so as a child my knowledge of Jesus was minimal. It was my best friend Jim, from middle school, who first invited me to church. He and his family introduced me to Jesus. After attending church with them for several months, I saw my need for a Savior. It was then that I began seeing some dramatic change in my life.

Like many new believers, I was excited about evangelism (a.k.a. preaching the gospel). My friends called me a "preaching machine." I became the president of our school's Bible club. I would gather crowds in the cafeteria during lunch hour to share the gospel, and I often started debates with my friends of other religions. I would frequently walk through the hallways before and after school praying for my classmates—laying hands on the lockers, asking God to bring revival to my high school.

At first, I was driven by the fact that I loved my classmates. It was common for my prayers to be mixed with tears for them. I wanted them to experience the same grace of God that I had experienced. But somewhere along the way, my motivations changed. My "preachiness" shifted. I went from being a loving preacher to being judgmental and self-righteous.

My preaching was no longer the result of wanting my classmates to experience the grace of God, but rather because I felt they needed to stop sinning. When I first became a Christian, I understood myself as a sinner in desperate need of God's love and grace. But somewhere along the way, I started to see myself as "holier than others."

This evolution in my heart was slow. It probably took about two years. By the time I was an upperclassman in high school, I misguidedly believed I was more valuable than everyone else simply because I believed I sinned less. I worked hard at my job, I tithed at least 10% of my money, I never cussed, I didn't drink or do drugs, I memorized Scripture, and I served as one of the key leaders in my youth group. I had developed this attitude that "God sure is lucky to have me on his team!"

I had somehow begun to believe that I had earned God's love. I don't think I would have ever said it that way, but as I look back, that's how I felt. And I secretly began to believe that others really just needed to be more like me. As I developed personal convictions and opinions, I would share them with others. And if they refused to embrace my opinion and convictions, I would bully them into admitting that they were wrong. There was one instance when some of my friends were listening to electronic music with no lyrics. I started berating them because they were listening to "worldly" music. If music did not overtly sing about Jesus, it was unacceptable to me. I often went out of my way to make people feel like they were bad Christians if they didn't embrace my opinions.

This dramatically changed one day during my senior year of high school.

I was sharing the gospel with my mother, as I had done many times before. And, also like many other instances, the discussion became quite heated. I had been trying to convince her that the Bible was authoritative and relevant to our lives, but the conversation shifted. At some point I began lashing out at her for not having raised me as a Christian. I then accused her of not being as good of a person as me. My mother was clearly not pleased. She felt disrespected. She then looked at me and said, "Well, maybe you should stop looking at porn every night. You think you're so much better than everyone, but you're a worse sinner than anyone else in this house."

You see, even though I had wanted to project the persona of being very holy, I actually had a dark secret—a secret addiction to pornography.

It was the 1990s. We didn't have smartphone devices. So I would use our family computer in the living room, but I'd do so late at night after my parents had gone to bed. Although I knew pornography was sinful—and I often experienced shame afterward—I had convinced myself that all of the other good things I did outweighed this one secret sin. I did not know that my mother had installed a software to track what I was doing. She had known for several weeks. She had been looking for the moment to drop the hammer. And she found the opportune time.

I was stunned. I fell silent. There were probably just a few seconds of silence and eye contact between us, but it felt like forever.

I was humiliated, ashamed. All of the sudden it hit me like a ton of bricks. I said nothing. I slowly walked away, went to my bedroom, and cried. I went back to my mother a few hours later and apologized. She was gracious and kind to me; we were able to talk through it. But the shame had already set in. A few days later a friend of mine said, "Kenny, you're down! You're not the same person!" I shrugged it off and assured him I was fine. But I wasn't fine. I felt depressed. My guilt and shame overwhelmed me for several months. The preaching machine had been silenced.

I struggled to read my Bible and pray. I'd grab my Bible and try to open it from time to time, but I just felt too ashamed.

THE JESUS I WISH I KNEW IN HIGH SCHOOL

I wish I had known in that moment with my mother, and during the next season of overwhelming sadness and shame, that Jesus loved me. I wish I had known that his arms were ready to embrace me.

Over the next few months, I slowly slipped out of that depression. I eventually began reading my Bible and praying again. I started to enjoy and re-engage in the Christian life, but it wasn't quite the same. I still had this wound, this sense that I was dirty. I was certainly no longer the self-righteous or judgmental person I had been for several years in high school, but I was truly struggling with any sense of confidence or assurance.

I went to Bible college after high school. There I started to study the book of Romans. It was this study that would transform my life. I began to study a doctrine known as "the imputation of righteousness." Basically, this means that the righteousness of Jesus is imputed (transferred or given) to us.

Let me explain this doctrine in simple terms. Imagine at the end of the semester you've got mostly Ds and Fs in all your classes. But someone else got straight As. Now imagine if that person opted to switch grades with you. Imagine you got all the credit for their good grades, and your bad grades were transferred to that person's record. In essence, this is exactly what Jesus did for us on the cross. He took on our sins and died the death we deserved.

Without Jesus, we all have "failing grades" in the ledgers of heaven. The Bible is clear that in our natural state, we are all absolute spiritual failures. God has set a standard of goodness and holiness; without Jesus we fail to meet that standard (most of us, with flying colors): "For all have sinned and fall short of the glory of God" (Romans 3:23). Each and every one of us have sinned. Our spiritual grades reflect that we have all failed.

But when we become followers of Jesus, he changes everything. His record is perfect. He lived the life you and I could not live even if we tried. And if you put your faith in Christ, he swaps his record with yours. You get credit for his work. You get *his* straight As.

Through Christ, our own records have been removed from us and Christ's record has been transferred to us. The great sixteenth-century pastor Martin Luther called this "the wonderful exchange."[1]

1. Martin Luther, quoted in J. I. Packer and Mark Dever, *In My Place Condemned He Stood* (Wheaton, IL: Crossway, 2008), 85.

I wish I had known in high school that not only was my sinful record—past, present, and future—completely eradicated, fully expunged, and wholly erased, but I was also declared righteous before God.

In studying the book of Romans, my eyes were awakened to this incredible truth: Jesus had chosen to forget my past, he wiped the record clean. I began to realize that I was declared righteous before God, not by my good behavior, but by Christ himself.

In Romans 4, the apostle Paul uses the Jewish patriarch Abraham as an example. He makes it clear that Abraham was declared righteous by God because of his belief in God, not by actions or works or behavior. Abraham gained favor with God, not because he made himself into a righteous man, but because he believed God. In his letter to the church in Corinth, Paul says, "that in him we might become the righteousness of God" (2 Corinthians 5:21b).

As I began to understand this truth, it transformed my life. During that previous season of shame, I would tell myself over and over again how I was too dirty and unworthy to pray. I remember lying in bed staring at the ceiling and wanting to pray, but I would say to myself, "Kenny, you've sinned way too much this week. God does not want to listen to you."

There were times when I'd enter into a corporate worship gathering or church service, but I wouldn't sing or engage. I'd just stand there, while everyone around me sang and praised God. I just felt like God didn't want to hear from me. I felt that I wasn't "good enough." But when I finally realized that because of Jesus, I was in right standing with God—that I had been declared righteous, that my heavenly record did not reflect my own folly, but instead reflected the righteousness of Jesus— God drew me to engage with him. I could come to him, knowing I had a clean record, not because of anything I had done, but because of what Christ had done on my behalf.

When I had given my faith to Christ several years earlier in middle school, it was that trust that made me righteous. Nothing else.

This truth transformed how I viewed others. No longer could I behave as if I were more righteous than other Christians. Christ is my only claim to righteousness.

This doctrine also shifted how I fought against my own sinful habits. I realized that I was no longer fighting against my sin to change God's opinion of me—his opinion of me was settled. I fight against sin because I love God, not because I'm earning my place in his family.

Whether I sin little or much, my place in God's family is not in jeopardy. Even when I sin, I can still come to God, sing to him, pray, and repent; I can do all this with confidence that he will listen and have mercy on me. In fact, the best thing I can do whenever I sin is to come to God, confess, and pray—knowing that my place with him is secure.

THE JESUS I WANT YOU TO KNOW

The gospel I wish I knew in high school is simply this: I am declared righteous before God because of my faith. Not because of anything I do or do not do.

And the same is true for you. If you have believed in Jesus, you are righteous. We fight against sin, not because we are earning our way to Jesus, but because of the joy set before us—that we have already been declared righteous in Christ.

DEVOTIONAL QUESTIONS

Read Romans 4:1–8.

1. How does Abraham become righteous? According to this passage, does Paul regard righteousness as a gift or an achievement?

2. The author of chapter 27 describes how he looked down on the sin of others. How does the gospel free us from arrogance and lead us toward humility and compassion?

3. Who are some people in your life you view as "worse sinners" than you? How might the gospel enable you to view them with compassion and humility?

RIGHTEOUSNESS (noun): The state of being perfectly acceptable to God in every way. Through Christ, sinners are counted as righteous before God. Another way to say it is, *you are enough.*

What this means for you: Because of Jesus, you are counted righteous before the God of the universe. You no longer have to try to prove yourself to him or others.

Chapter 28
Tragedy and Healing
by Scotty Smith

My earliest impressions of Jesus are connected to two distinct environments: the church of my childhood, and my maternal grandparents' home in Charlotte, North Carolina.

Our family attended a church I would describe as "southern." As a faith community, we didn't fight liberals, or conservatives; we just "went to church." It's just what you did on Sunday morning. I was born in 1950 and the question, "Where do y'all go to church?" was as common as "Where do you grocery shop?" or "Can you recommend a family doctor?" or "Who can I trust to fix my car?" or "What do y'all do for fun?"

But I went to *church* long before I went to *Christ*. Mine was an assumed gospel; not a needed or celebrated one. Whenever I thought of Jesus, I imagined a rather tall, light-skinned man, with long shiny brunette hair. He wore an off-white robe with no wrinkles in it. He was surrounded by lambs and crowds of people.

I certainly thought of Jesus as an important role model, though I didn't consciously try to follow him. Nor did I have any concept of having a relationship with him. I believed all you had to do to go to heaven was die. I wasn't afraid of God or hell, and I didn't live with a particularly guilty conscience. I was taught good and bad, but I simply ignored God most of the time, except for a few religious superstitions.

For instance, I would say a prayer of forgiveness and protection most nights at bedtime. Occasionally I would shoot up some "bartering" prayers to God: "Please get me out of this mess, and I'll do better." And we did repeat a "blessing" before we ate supper as a family. I would never think of setting anything on top of the Bible that collected dust in the headboard-bookcase of my twin bed. And I zealously sought never to utter any word damning God's name. But I never read the Bible; God's name was simply a three-letter word.

My exposure to God, Jesus, and spirituality took a different shape in Grandmother and Granddaddy Ward's home. Whenever I spent the night at their home (a great treat)—after a most wonderful breakfast, my grandparents would take a little Bible verse from a plastic loaf of bread, read it, and then take a few minutes to pray for all of us—their five adult children and their many grandkids. They prayed. They loved. They talked to God in personal, endearing, and comforting ways.

When I came to faith in Christ during my senior year of high school, I found language to describe their beautiful relationship with God. They offered up the "aroma of Christ" as described by the apostle Paul in 2 Corinthians 2:15–16. I saw the gospel of God's grace in them before I ever knew my need for it.

My grandparents "beautified" the gospel with their tears, welcome, and kindness. They struggled honestly and valiantly in life. For years, my granddaddy bravely suffered through severe depression, and they both loved my aunt through a ten-year heroin addiction. But the next tragedy to interrupt their lives devastated mine as well. When I was eleven years old, my mom—their daughter—was killed in a head-on car wreck.

The tragedy of my mom's death exposed several things in my life: the absence of my relationship with Jesus, the absence of a relationship with my dad, and how much I relied on my mom. She was my world—my oxygen, light, and feast. My dad was essentially a stranger. He paid the bills, but he didn't act like a father. We didn't touch, and rarely talked. Our distant relationship continued for years after the death of my mom. From the age of eleven through eighteen, I felt like a housed, but homeless child.

Three years before my mom died, a part of me died as well. I was lured into a neighbor's barn, where an older boy I admired sexually abused me. Thankfully, this didn't begin a systemic cycle of abuse. It only happened once; but with enough impact to break and skew how I viewed sex, sexuality, and my body. Perhaps due in part to the hyper-masculine messages I'd received from my father, I never shared this story with anyone until many years later. I wish I had known that Jesus invited me to come with my shame, and to find healing.

Through those difficult years, I masked my pain and insecurities with food, attention from others, and alcohol. They became my temporary, insufficient healers.

But things changed in 1968. At the age of eighteen, I came to know Jesus personally at a Billy Graham movie event—*The Restless Ones*. Bad acting, poor script, cheesy music, but when Dr. Graham presented the good news of Jesus, I heard the gospel in a way I had never heard before. I consciously received the free gift of eternal life. I truly believed Jesus lived, died, and rose again for me.

For six decades, I have trusted that there's nothing more than the gospel, just *more of it*. God continues to expose my deepest needs and affirm his absolute sufficiency to meet them.

THE JESUS I WISH I KNEW IN HIGH SCHOOL

In high school, I wish I had known that Jesus is a Savior to love and trust, not simply a model to follow. My initial understanding of the gospel went something like this: once you become a follower of Jesus, all your sins—past, present, and future—are forgiven. In gratitude, you fill your life with good works.

Though I didn't base my salvation on good works—I did take pride in my "goodness." I confused pleasing Jesus with appeasing Jesus. I wanted to keep him happy.

It took years for me to discover that my works can never earn his happiness. When Jesus died for my sins on the cross, he completely satisfied my sin-debt for all eternity. He covered me with his perfect righteousness. He came to be my Savior for always—even on the dark days. I wish I had understood how much more of Jesus there was to see and savor. God has been faithful these many years to expose the much-more-ness of my need, and the way-much-more-ness of Jesus.

In high school, I wish I had known Jesus as my healer. Isaiah 53:5b says, "with his wounds we are healed." As a child, I was told to be strong. I didn't need healing. I wasn't sick. I wasn't needy. My dad modeled the concept, *big boys don't cry*. So I didn't.

This message, clouded with the misguided concept of Christian victory (see Romans 8:28), left little room for me to honestly process my grief. I thought I was to be "more than a conqueror" in life. So I masked my pain. I hid my grief.

What I really needed then and continue to need now, is the freedom to live honestly and transparently. Christ welcomes us to come. He is with us and *for* us in our pain and sorrow. He wants to join us in these difficult places. We have no reason to hide; we are welcome.

I wish I had known as a teenager that God enters our brokenness; he brings tender presence and healing grace. He weeps over death and abuse and he carries our shame.

I wish I had known that in the absence of love from my own earthly father, Jesus reveals the Father to us, that we might be re-parented through the Spirit of adoption.

To see Jesus is to see the Father, which doesn't mean Jesus *is* the Father. It means, as the Son of God, Jesus perfectly reveals the family likeness. It also means that by his life, death, and resurrection, Jesus has done everything necessary for us to become daughters and sons of the living God. To receive Jesus is to be given the legal rights and personal delights of having God as our Father.

By the riches of grace and the Spirit's work, we learn to cry "Abba, Father." It's the cry of desperation and delight, vulnerability and surrender, honesty and hope. As we grow as his children, we come alive to the love and presence of the only perfect parent. Oh, how I wish I had known God as the Father of mercies and God of all comfort in high school.

THE JESUS I WANT YOU TO KNOW

My friends, I want you to know God's welcome is always primed to receive you. His grace is completely inexhaustible, no matter your struggles or brokenness. His mercies will always overmatch your messes. And his love for you is the greatest constant and freedom you will ever experience in life. I so wish I had believed this in high school; but I'm grateful to believe it now and always.

DEVOTIONAL QUESTIONS

Read Isaiah 52:1–13.

1. Isaiah 52 prophetically describes Jesus. Which phrases encourage you to trust Jesus with your weakness?
2. The author of chapter 28 shares how he learned to hide his hurt and pain. Have you ever been discouraged from sharing honestly?
3. How can God's grace and the person of Jesus enable you to be more open and honest about your own struggles, sins, and fears?

EMMANUEL (proper noun): A Hebrew word meaning, "God with us." In the book of Matthew, we learn that Jesus himself is our Emmanuel.

What this means for you: As New York pastor Tim Keller has noted, most world religions tell you how you can get to God; but Jesus is the God who came to be with you. Jesus is the God who ate with sinners and touched the ill. On the cross, he shows you that he isn't just *with you*, he is *for you*.

Chapter 29
Regret and Rescue
by Lucy Kate Green

I n the climax of the movie *The Edge of Seventeen,*[1] the main character (who is angsty, bored, frustrated, and lonely) claims that she watches herself do or say terrible things to her friends and family, hates herself for doing or saying those things, and fears tremendously that she will never be able to change.

I, too, spent much of high school doing and saying terrible things, and consequently hating myself for them.

I instigated gossip, betrayed friends, constantly fought with my parents, neglected school, and drank myself sick. I hated myself for doing these things, yet I didn't change my behavior because somewhere deep down I believed that God hated who I was, too. As a teenager, I really believed that it didn't matter what I did, because I'd already lost the impossible contest for God's approval. I could never atone for the qualities about myself that caused him to hold his nose when he watched me go about my life.

Part of this was natural and not a result of any particular event. I have a tendency to be a legalist; even as a young kid, I didn't know what to do with feelings of guilt other than assume

---

1. *The Edge of Seventeen,* directed by Kelly Fremon Craig (2016; Burbank, CA: STX Entertainment, 2016), DVD.

that God *wanted* me to feel guilty. In kindergarten, a boy in my class kissed me unexpectedly at the playground. I had a knot in my stomach for weeks when I would go to church because I was convinced that God couldn't accept me now. How silly, I know, that a six-year-old would have such a great assumption about God's feelings!

But I sensed that there was something perfect about God, something unacceptable about myself, and an irreparable abyss in the middle.

As high school rolled around, I bounced from guy to guy—each week focusing my eyes on someone different—hoping they'd approve of me, uplift me, and replace the nagging sense that I was not enough. Each time I hoped that their acceptance and approval would make me *feel* accepted and approved of, but it never did. With each new guy, my sense of guilt, fear, and disapproval only grew.

Going through boys eventually wasn't enough, so I dove into the world of alcohol. My perception of God's anger only grew as I saw my sin more acutely. I distinctly remember this at a party my junior year. I don't remember much from that night except for a friend sticking her fingers down my throat out of fear that I would have to go to the hospital because of the amount of tequila I drank. I spent much of the night on the bathroom floor, then moved into the bedroom. Early that morning, I woke up squished between boys. I distinctly remember crying, staring at the ceiling which spun above me, devastated that God could see me like this. I imagined him being furious, disappointed, and silent. Just one more thing on my already tarnished record.

In that moment, I felt like I was waving goodbye to someone who had no choice but to walk away from me.

Though I didn't have the theological knowledge then to understand it, my teenage years were a clear picture of a life without Jesus. I was keenly aware that I was separated from God. I knew I fell terribly short of his standards. I knew that the gap between us was too wide. I knew I had no control.

What I know now is that Jesus was the solution to my deep, painful feelings—he was the bridge that would unite God to myself.

THE JESUS I WISH I KNEW IN HIGH SCHOOL

Growing up, I believed that people were basically good and that I must have been the exception; I felt like a fraud, and I spun out trying to avoid that feeling. I wish I'd known that we are not born perfect. Instead, we are born in sin and selfishness, and any turning from our self-serving plans and desires is a miraculous work of the Spirit. Every one of us is born with a rotten track record, and we aren't capable of anything more. I wish I'd understood this in high school. The sinful behaviors, guilt, and distance from God had come as a surprise to me, and so I assumed they came as a surprise to God, too.

The Jesus I wish I knew in high school is simple: I wish I'd known that he was not remotely surprised by my falling short, and that the reason he came to earth was to die on the cross for my sins—to bring me across that awful abyss of my sin into the arms of this perfect God.

This truth is proven countless times in Scripture. In Romans 5:8b, Paul writes that "while we were still sinners, Christ died for us." In Matthew 7:11, Jesus reassures his disciples that their Father in heaven knows that they are evil, and yet loves to give them good gifts. Throughout Peter's life, we see a shaky disciple who denies the crucified Jesus three times. Not only was Jesus not surprised by this betrayal, Jesus actually told Peter it would happen. During all three years they spent together, Jesus knew that Peter would not be strong enough to stand by him. Yet Jesus also told Peter that his confession would be the rock on which Jesus builds his church—and it was (see Acts 10).

Jesus wasn't surprised by the failings of those around him, and he certainly isn't surprised when I fall short. Even though he is a holy, all-knowing God, he is delighted when sinners draw near to him. He is not mad at them, nor was he mad at me. His heart and mission is to rescue sinners.

The basic truth that Jesus came to earth to pay for my sin, is half of what I wish I'd known in high school. I also needed to know the deeper truth, that Jesus came to earth as a radical declaration of God's unwillingness to live without me. Like Thomas Torrance says, "There is no hidden God behind the back of Jesus."[2] God was not mad at me; he was in love with me. He created me so that he could spend forever loving me, and he died to show me this love. He doesn't need my life to be a decent offering—he offered everything for me regardless of what I've done (and regardless of what I will do!), all for the joy of having me in his arms (see Hebrews 12:2).

This joy must be the focus of your existence. Not behavior that is pious or worthy, but joy in knowing that you are breathing because he loves you. He wants to love away the guilt, the hurt, the slavery, and the disgust you feel with yourself. When you feel at your very worst, certain that God's love has already expired, envision him running toward the cross to bring you back home. This is the truth; this is your reality.

I am the drunk sixteen-year-old who kissed too many boys. And I am now a twenty-four-year-old youth minister in Birmingham, Alabama. While I am still a sinner, I no longer wince at the thought of God's anger toward me—instead I run toward the God who loves me—the One who left heaven to rescue me.

THE JESUS I WANT YOU TO KNOW

If you are living with regrets and feel like it's too late; if you're afraid of the God who sees all; if you long for a relationship with Jesus, but have no idea where to start, hear this:

He is not surprised by your screwups, and his voice is radically different from those of your peers or your parents or yourself. He doesn't want you to start behaving better, he wants you to know that you are deeply loved, free, and redeemed.

---

2. Thomas Torrance, *The Christian Doctrine of God, One Being Three Persons* (New York: T & T Clark, 2001), 243–44.

When I was in high school staring at the spinning ceiling, God didn't just forgive me and then hope I'd get back on track. He was with me in that very moment, telling me there was nothing I could do to make him stop loving me, and nothing I could do to make him love me more. He is with you, he will save you, and he rejoices over you (see Zephaniah 3:17). The open arms of Jesus are a message to you—he is not mad at you. The cross is there to prove it.

DEVOTIONAL QUESTIONS

Read Romans 5:8.

1. What does this passage reveal about God's knowledge of your sin? What has he done in response?
2. The author of chapter 29 describes how she envisioned God's disapproval. How did this influence her behavior and choices?
3. How do you think God feels about you when you make mistakes? How do you think God feels about you in general? How might this influence your choices?

OMNIPOTENCE (noun): Having unlimited power, able to do anything. In the biblical sense, this is who God is.

What this means for you: You are loved by a mighty and all-powerful God. He can do anything, be in all places, knows absolutely everything, and has plans for you to prosper. When tragedy or challenges enter your life, you can be certain God is in control, and that he turns all things—even the worst things—toward good. Whatever you are dealing with right now, this omnipotent God is with you, he is not surprised by your circumstances, and he is already making a way through it.

Chapter 30
Isolation and Liberation
by Clark Fobes IV

"**T**hey can never know."

"I will take this with me to my grave."

"If they really knew who I was, they would never love or accept me."

I was raised in a non-Christian home in the liberal city of San Francisco. Christianity was not the norm. Choosing to follow Jesus meant counting the cost of what my family and friends would think of me, and consciously choosing Jesus over the world. When I eventually did come to Christ, I was convinced that he was the answer to my questions and longings.

Despite this certainty, I faced an unresolved question. If I was so certain of my faith, so devoted to following Jesus, then why did I still struggle so deeply with sin? Why did I still feel the need to hide my sin—from God, from my youth leaders, from my friends? Why wasn't I experiencing true freedom—the kind I heard about at church?

For most of my high school years, these questions haunted me as I strained to live out my newfound convictions of faith and remain chaste in my pursuit of holiness—particularly in the area of lust and sexual relationships. As a teenage boy, I was convinced that none of my other "good" Christian friends were struggling as horribly as I was. Perhaps it was my non-Christian upbringing; maybe it was because I wasn't as committed to Jesus as I thought I was. Doubts regularly flooded my mind and as a result, I resolved to lock away this ugly part of my heart forever, never to be seen by anyone in the church.

The voices of shame assaulted me daily, telling me that if anybody knew who I really was, I would never be accepted; I had to hide. As much as I *knew* I was saved by grace, deemed holy and pure by Jesus's blood, and declared "justified"—no longer carrying the penalty for my sin—I also worried I was not living as a true Christ-follower. I might have been saved by grace, but my sin was just too shameful for grace to overcome.

The gospel was regularly preached in my youth group, and my youth leaders were committed to displaying the love and grace of Jesus to us; but despite their faithful efforts, something about the gospel still felt foreign. The language of "justification," "righteousness," and "victory" just didn't hit my heart in a way that allowed me to actually experience freedom from sin.

Jesus might have handled my sin and guilt on the cross, but my shame still prevailed. God might have forgiven me for my sins, but I still felt trapped by the pressure of measuring up to the expectations of those around me. The gospel proclaimed my salvation before God, but it didn't erase the shame I still experienced within my Asian-American community and upbringing.

Growing up half-Korean in a predominantly Asian setting, the individual themes of guilt and innocence were not prevalent. What was prevalent were the themes of a culture built around the common good for the group, and the honor or shame attached to my actions and how they affected that group. To be spoken highly of by others was of greater importance than being certain that I had followed all the rules. Doing everything right in my own conscience didn't matter if I did not have the approval and admiration of my family and friends. So while I inwardly believed the truth of the cross, I was outwardly still functioning according to the truth of my culture.

Would I ever experience the full freedom of the gospel? Either something was wrong with the gospel, or something was wrong with *me*. I had already lived a life without the gospel, so I was not willing to buy into the former; therefore, the problem must have been with me.

Ashamed of my inability to measure up to the Christian standard, and afraid of what my community would think of me, I resigned that I might never experience freedom from sin; this was a burden I would have to bear alone. Maybe, after enough years of following Jesus, or enough effort on my own part, freedom would finally come.

THE JESUS I WISH I KNEW IN HIGH SCHOOL

Entering college proved no easier; my struggle with lust did not go away, even though I was maturing in faith. In fact, it only got harder as many of my friends were now more sexually active than in high school, and my heart continued to burn for intimacy. It was in this state of internal turmoil that Jesus began meeting me and applying the gospel to my heart in ways that I had not experienced before.

While I received a solid biblical understanding of the gospel through my home church, it was through my church in college that the gospel finally started resonating with my heart. I knew in my head that I was justified—saved by grace and from no efforts of my own—but my culture still told me that my existence was justified by the prestige and honor bestowed by those around me. As a Christian I believed that it was only because of Christ's righteousness (not my own) that I could stand before God, but my cultural experience upheld that I was only blameless if I measured up to others' expectations of me as a son, friend, and student.

With great cultural awareness, the pastors and members of that small church in college helped me realize that God's approval of me wasn't bound to my efforts for him, but in Christ's efforts already accomplished for me. No amount of prestige, honor, or affirmation from others would ever allow me to measure up to Jesus, the perfect Son who—by the world's standards—God *should* have always been comparing me to (for any Asian readers, we know that there is always a "better sibling/cousin/friend" whom we despised for making us look bad).

Instead, through Christ's sacrifice, God now bestowed on me the very honor of Jesus, giving me all of the prestige and affirmation that was reserved for him.

Not only was this culturally relevant gospel preached at my church in college, it was also demonstrated in love as people shared honestly and vulnerably with one another. Sins were openly confessed and transparency was encouraged; instead of being reprimanded for showing weakness or being shunned for our imperfections, love was extended with the verbal embrace of Christ and the physical embrace of fellow believers. Though sin was still present in my life, I experienced victory in Christ in such a way that shame no longer had a hold on me.

I finally understood that "freedom" and "victory" didn't mean I would never sin again, but that Jesus had liberated me from the need to constantly examine myself in vain attempts to display perfection to the world. Jesus had met me in ways that went beyond my theological understanding of the gospel. He led me into a deeper, more personal, and even culturally specific way that hit my heart with the healing dagger of grace.

Before, I felt like the woman at the well whom Jesus encounters in John 4, anxiously hiding my true self from my community—trapped in isolation by the shame of my own temptations and sin. Like this woman, I dreaded the exposure of my true self and struggles. I hid at all costs. I made every effort to cover myself with more religious activity.

But thankfully, like this woman, Jesus also met me with the bold audacity of his gentle grace. Now, like this woman, I came to experience freedom, to the point where I could run to my village and publicly declare, "Come, see a man who told me all that I ever did" (John 4:29)—as in, the string of men she had been sleeping with in pursuit of living water. Like her, I experienced true freedom in the person of Jesus Christ. The exposure of my sin before others was no longer an act of shame, but of honor—exalting Christ and his wondrous gospel.

I wish I could return to my younger high school-self and speak this message of freedom and peace. I wish I could point him to the love and approval he already had in God the Father. I wish I could convey to him how true freedom is not the absence of sin, but the absence of sin's shameful hold. I wish I could have experienced the liberating effects of encountering Jesus—freeing me from the constant need of approval and affirmation from others.

Though I can't go back in time to speak these words to my younger self, I have the privilege of speaking them to you, beloved brother and sister, right now.

THE JESUS I WANT YOU TO KNOW

Whether you are from a culture that values honor and affirmation from others, or you are a teen overwhelmed by the pressure to measure up to others' opinions of you on social media, I want you to know that only in Jesus—in the multifaceted gospel that reaches all cultures—will you find full freedom. As you labor and toil to daily find approval from friends through tangible "Likes," or to be recognized and praised by your family, how I hope you will see the vain and fleeting nature of these endless pursuits. How I hope you will truly believe that the only lasting approval comes at the hands of a God who subjected his own Son to shame and dishonor for your sake.

You might feel like me, like the woman at the well, isolated and ashamed because of your sin; but I also hope you share in our experience with Jesus—of being fully known and accepted, radically loved, finally free. A life that has been deeply met with the bold grace of Christ is a life that is free to go and tell others "all that I ever did," because we know that our only security is found not in the praise and approval from the world, but in the affirmation from a King. Like the Samaritan woman, may we leave our jars for drawing water at the well, and run to the living water we find at the cross.

DEVOTIONAL QUESTIONS

Read John 4:1–30.

1. What does Jesus already know about the woman? How does he treat her, in light of what he already knows?
2. The author of chapter 30 describes his struggle to find freedom from sin in light of his culture and community. Is there a particular sin in your own life that causes you to hide from others?
3. What would need to happen in order for you to find full freedom from that sin, before God and others? Knowing that Jesus knows every single thing about you, can you accept the reality that you are radically loved? How can you begin to experience and live out this freedom of the gospel today?

LIBERATION (noun): When Christ redeems his people, he also frees them from sin's hold and effects. Liberation will not fully be experienced until the new heavens and new earth, but the freedom from sin found in the gospel—individual and systemic—can be seen and felt in glimpses today.

What this means for you: You may at times feel defeated and discouraged by your own sin, and the sin you see around you in the world. The gospel means that you can experience real freedom today, while you also hope for a future liberation of all of creation, when all sin will be done away with.

Glossary

adoption (noun). When a person puts their faith in Christ, they are adopted as a child of God. As his child, they receive all the benefits of being an heir of the King. (p. 37)

approval (noun). The belief that someone or something is good or acceptable. (p. 49)

Emmanuel (proper noun). A Hebrew word meaning, "God with us." In the book of Matthew, we learn that Jesus himself is our Emmanuel. (p. 168)

enoughness (noun). The reality that you lack nothing. (p. 83)

freedom (noun). Being released from eternal death, bondage to sin, and the need to prove ourselves. (p. 144)

grace (noun). God's underserved love and favor for sinners through Christ. (p. 54)

hidden in Christ (adjective). On the cross, Jesus was "clothed in our shame, crowned with our thorns, and exposed to the judgment of God that we deserve."[1] On the cross, there was no place for Jesus to hide; he became our hiding place. (p. 125)

---

1. Eric Watkins, "Hidden with Christ," Ligonier Ministries: the teaching fellowship of R. C. Sproul, 2014, https://www.ligonier.org/learn/devotionals/hidden-with-christ/.

human being vs. human doing (nouns). Many people believe that their worth is found in *doing* (actions and achievements). But worth is actually found in *being* created in God's image, formed by his love. (p. 65)

identity in Christ (noun). Who you are is based on who Christ is. (p. 43)

idolatry (noun). Ascribing value to things of this world that should actually be assigned to God himself. Examples might include viewing money, success, or popularity as equal to God. (p. 71)

incarnation (noun). The event when God came down to earth and took on human flesh in the person of Jesus. (p. 26)

justification (noun). The two-fold process whereby a person's sins are forgiven and they, through faith, receive the perfect righteousness of Christ. (p. 31)

liberation (noun). When Christ redeems his people, he also frees them from sin's hold and effects. Liberation will not fully be experienced until the new heavens and new earth, but the freedom found in the gospel from sin—individual and systemic—can be seen and felt in glimpses today. (p. 179)

Man of Sorrows (proper noun). Isaiah 53:3a predicts that many years before the birth of Christ, the Messiah would be "despised and rejected by men, a man of sorrows and acquainted with grief." (p. 113)

new heavens/new earth (nouns). At the end of time, Christ will return to the earth, and all will be made perfect. The heavens and earth will join together as one, like Eden. (p. 95)

new life (noun). When Christ saves us, he transfers us from death and darkness into life and light. The joy and peace we experience as Christians is evidence of this transfer to new life. (p. 119)

omnipotence (noun). Having unlimited power, able to do anything. In the biblical sense, this is who God is. (p. 173)

performance (noun). Accomplishing or fulfilling an act, task, or function. (p. 101)

redemption (noun). In the Bible, redemption refers to crossing over from one thing to another. When Jesus redeems a person, he alters them from darkness to light, from death to life, from an enemy of God to a child of God, from judgment to eternal life. (p. 131)

rest (noun). Freedom from striving. When a person is made righteous by Christ, they no longer have to prove themselves. They can rest in God's grace and Christ's work. (p. 77)

righteousness (noun). The state of being perfectly acceptable to God in every way. Through Christ, sinners are counted as righteous before God. Another way to say it is, *you are enough.* (p. 163)

sin (noun). 1) Disobeying God's commands (behavioral), 2) Desiring to be the god of your own life (theological), 3) Separation from God (relational). (p. 59)

surrender (verb). To release control completely. To give in to the power of another. (p. 8)

sympathy vs. empathy (nouns). Having sympathy involves having compassion for another person, even though you can't identify with their suffering. Having empathy involves compassion *with* understanding. It is a shared experience. (p. 20)

the body of Christ (noun). This is the worldwide church, Christ's hands and feet on earth—you, me, and our various local churches and Christian organizations. (p. 156)

the gospel (noun). The good news of God's grace and redemption for sinners through the life, death, and resurrection of Jesus Christ. It is the primary message of the Bible and of Christianity. (p. 14)

the honor/shame worldview (noun). Honor/Shame is a way that many cultures see the world. Honor is given to people who act in line with a shared social code; anyone who fails to live up to that code has shame placed upon them. We see this most often in social media interactions, where we have to be careful what we post, lest we get "cancelled." This worldview can sometimes curb bad behavior, but it can also leave us feeling deeply unworthy. (p. 107)

the law (noun). The law often refers to God's commandments in the Bible. We can understand it as God's blueprints for human flourishing. Instead of trusting Jesus with our identity and worth, we often look to law-following to justify ourselves. But the law cannot give us life; the Holy Spirit is the One who gives us life. (p. 138)

transformation (or sanctification) (nouns). The process whereby a Christian grows in dependence on the grace of God. As they depend on God, the Lord changes them into a more Christlike person, although they will continue to struggle with sin. (p. 150)

worthy (noun). The reality that your life has value. (p. 89)

 **rooted** | ministry

Equipping and empowering churches and parents
to faithfully disciple teenagers toward
lifelong faith in Christ.

Check out our: Blog, Podcasts, Books, YouTube,
Regional Groups, Conference, Training, Curriculum

www.rootedministry.com

 **rooted** | reservoir

Your online source for gospel-centered
youth ministry training and curriculum

Bible-Based Curriculum, Training Videos,
Teaching Illustrations Bank, Online Community

www.rootedreservoir.com